Producing Music
with
Samples, Loops, and MIDI

The S.M.A.R.T. guide to

Bill Gibson

THOMSON

COURSE TECHNOLOGY

Professional ■ Technical ■ Reference

The S.M.A.R.T. Guide to Producing Music with Samples, Loops, and MIDI
by Bill Gibson

Publisher and General Manager, Thomson Course Technology PTR: Stacy L. Hiquet
Associate Director of Marketing: Sarah O'Donnell
Manager of Editorial Services: Heather Talbot
Marketing Manager: Cathleen D. Snyder
Executive Editor: Mike Lawson
Senior Editor: Mark Garvey
Marketing Coordinator: Jordan Casey
Project Editor and Copy Editor: Cathleen D. Snyder
Thomson Course Technology PTR Editorial Services Coordinator: Elizabeth Furbish
Cover Designer: Steve Ramirez
Indexer: Katherine Stimson

ISBN: 1-59200-697-3
Library of Congress Catalog Card Number: 2005927505
Printed in United States of America
05 06 07 08 09 BU 10 9 8 7 6 5 4 3 2

THOMSON
COURSE TECHNOLOGY
Professional ■ Technical ■ Reference

Thomson Course Technology PTR, a division of Thomson Course Technology
25 Thomson Place
Boston, MA 02210
http://www.courseptr.com

Dedication

This book is dedicated to my mother, Vera. Although you've been gone for many years, I still hear your encouraging words and feel your love.

Acknowledgements

To all the folks who have helped support the development and integrity of these books. Thank you for your continued support and interest in providing great tools for us all to use.

Acoustic Sciences, Inc.
Antares
Big Fish Audio
Digidesign
eLab
Gibson Guitars
LinPlug Virtual Instruments
Mackie
Mike Kay at Ted Brown Music in Tacoma, WA
Monster Cable
MOTU
Native Instruments
Primacoustic Studio Acoustics
Radial Engineering
Robbie Ott
Roger Wood
Sabian Cymbals
Shure
Spectrasonics
T.C. Electronic
Taye Drums
Universal Audio
Waves Plug-ins

About the Author

Bill Gibson, president of Northwest Music and Recording, has spent the last 25 years writing, recording, producing, and teaching music and has become well-known for his production, performance, and teaching skills. As an instructor at Green River College in Auburn, Washington, holding various degrees in composition, arranging, education, and recording, he developed a practical and accessible teaching style which provided the basis for what was to come—more than 20 books, a DVD, and a VHS video for MixBooks/ArtistPro, along with a dozen online courses for members of ArtistPro.com. Gibson's writings are acclaimed for their straightforward and understandable explanations of recording concepts and applications.

Introduction

The S.M.A.R.T. Guide to Producing Music with Samples, Loops, and MIDI. The
title stands for Serious Music and Audio Recording Techniques, and everything
contained in this series is designed to help you learn to capture seriously great sound and
music. These books are written by a producer/engineer with a degree in composition
and arranging, not in electronics. All explanations are straightforward and pragmatic.
If you're a regular person who loves music and wants to produce recordings that hold
their own in the marketplace, these books are definitely written just for you. If you're
a student of the recording process, the explanations contained in these books could
be some of the most enlightening and easy to understand that you'll find. In addition,
the audio and video examples on the accompanying DVD were produced in a direct
and simple manner. Each of these examples delivers content that's rich with meaning,
accessible, and very pertinent to the process of learning to record great-sounding audio.

Contents

Chapter 3 - Sampling 59

Chapter 4 - Rhythm Section and Vocal Sampling 93

Chapter 6 - Building Custom Loops.................................147

Chapter 8 - MIDI Production Techniques

Audio and Video Examples

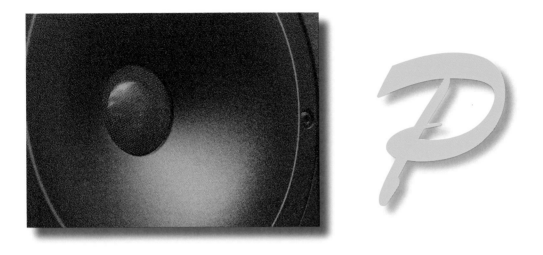

Preface

W elcome to the fourth book in the *S.M.A.R.T. Guide* series from Thomson Course PTR. This edition is packed with information you need to know about the creative use of samples, loops, and MIDI. Learn some tested techniques for creating high-quality music using modern technology. If you enjoy great music and appreciate creativity, emotion, and passion, you must gain experience in producing music with these valuable tools.

The topics covered in this book are very important in music production today. Even though a sampler is essentially a digital recorder, there are capabilities and functionalities available in hardware or software samplers that are unique and powerful. Learn these features and see how they're used.

Samples and loops are identical in many ways, yet functionally different in many ways. Samples are often played once—they are more of a "one shot" tool. Loops are constructed to be played over and over, while

timing and the groove remain perfectly smooth. There are special considerations when working with loops that will help you produce music that
is powerful, thought provoking, authentic, and compelling.

MIDI became an integral part of music production in the 1980s.
It has remained an important part of the recording process throughout
the years, but the acceptance of purely computerized music has waned.
Modern listeners expect to hear music that has emotion, authenticity,
and great rhythmic feel. Combining MIDI sequencing with excellent
instrumentals and vocals takes advantage of the best of each technical
process. MIDI protocol contains ample parameters and controls to
allow the production of music that retains much of the realism of
the musician's performance as he or she plays the keyboard or other
triggering device capable of entering MIDI information into the MIDI
sequence.

The explanations and examples in this book will help you, whether
you're operating in your home studio or in a professional recording
facility. There is so much involved with music production. The more
types of technologies you incorporate in your productions, the greater
your depth of understanding should be. You must know enough about
your tools to get the most out of them in the pursuit of high-quality
musical productions. We are in an age where technological advances
are commonplace—often, they seem to happen on a daily basis. The
information in this book will help you optimize your current setup,
and it just might reveal some tools that you can add to your system in
order to increase your productivity. In addition, the topics covered in
this book hold great potential for supporting the artistic and creative
vision, which is yours alone.

It's exciting that our tools are getting better and better. The good
news is that almost anyone can develop a system capable of producing

hit-quality audio—that's also the bad news. If you're going to have an edge in an increasingly competitive industry like music and audio, you must get both your technical and artistic act together. It's imperative. In the professional music and recording world, we all need to continually increase our skill and knowledge—the process of repeatedly taking what we're capable of to the next level is both mandatory and exhilarating at the same time.

Be sure to listen to and watch the enclosed DVD. The Audio Examples demonstrate many of the concepts that are explained in the text and accompanying illustrations. The Video Examples show you specifically how to optimize your recordings in crucial musical situations. Instructionally, they are very powerful. These video clips are produced with your education in mind. You won't find a lot of rapid-motion, highly stylized shots; you will find easy-to-understand instructional video that is edited for optimal instruction and learning.

Audio Examples are indicated like this.

Video Examples are indicated like this.

I'm excited to share this information with you. Samples, loops, and MIDI are a huge part of the recording world as it functions today. However, the exciting part of our industry is that almost any manufacturer might be about to release a technology that's going to change everything! Personally, I can't wait. I've known for some time that I love the constant opportunity to learn—it is so fundamental to the recording process. If everything was the same as when I started recording, not only would it have gotten a bit technologically boring, but gear would be prohibitively expensive for the entry-level recordist, who might be the one about to revolutionize the creative process. Creativity is always enjoyable. However, the creative freedom that we now realize in the audio industry is amazing!

Have fun! Keep the vision alive!

Sampler History

In its most basic form, a sampler is simply a device that records a sound. In the early days of recording, samples were taken of previously recorded music and reconstructed into other musical compositions. These samples were typically reconstructed from the original media, such as tape or vinyl.

Introduction

Today, our definition of a sampler has been refined to include a digital recorder that is controlled from a MIDI device. In our previous discussions of the digital recording process (*The S.M.A.R.T Guide to Digital Recording, Software, and Plug-Ins*), you learned that a sample is a binary representation of a sound wave's amplitude at a specific point in time. Several of these binary "snapshots" combine along the timeline axis to digitally represent the analog waveform. Although these samples define the digital recording process, in the modern keyboard and recording world a sampler includes a MIDI keyboard that controls the pitch, attack velocities, controller parameters, and so on.

The MIDI parameter controls, such as pitch bend, LFO, volume, and so on, affect the digital samples. Also, the keys are typically, though not always, defined to raise and lower the pitch in half-step increments up and down the keyboard. Keep in mind that you get to choose how the MIDI controls actually affect the samples so it is entirely possible, and sometimes very cool, to set several keys on the keyboard to the same sample with the pitch remaining constant but the layering, attack, or filter options set differently. You get to choose how best to set up the MIDI system for your creative expression.

History

It's important to understand the history of sampling. In many ways, it parallels the history of digital recording use in the professional audio recording world. It is truly amazing just how relatively contemporary many of the tools we use are. Samplers, in their most basic form, appeared in the early 1980s. It's amazing how powerful the original samplers were in many respects and how sonically archaic they were in other respects.

As you read this chapter, absorb the information and observe the incredibly creative uses of the original samplers. Modern samplers and digital recorders are so powerful that music production is almost too easy. The complex problem solving and ingenuity that are required in a basic system are sometimes the impetus that drives creative thinking. Try to maintain your creative drive, even in the use of such powerful tools as we're using today.

Musique Concréte

Musique concréte provided the experimental foundation for the modern-day use of samples and loops in musical composition. In 1942, French writer, technical engineer, audio pioneer, and broadcaster

Schaeffer's 5-Track Setup

Schaeffer's 5-track playback system is amazingly close to any modern-day surround-sound system. It is especially amazing considering he developed the concept in the early 1950s. His roving live-performance fifth channel is rather ingenious in many ways, although modern control systems provide for exact imaging within any number of surround tracks.

In addition to the live microphone, Schaeffer's configuration included four stationary speakers positioned at front right, front left, center back, and directly overhead.

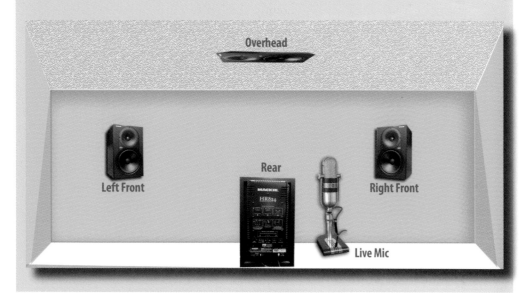

Pierre Schaeffer (1910 – 1995) created musique concréte, a compositional process that relied on natural sounds and the manipulation and editing of already existing recorded music. This compositional process did not rely on performances by musicians; rather, it relied on other recordings pieced together in a creative and musical way.

The original compositions were based on the manipulation of phonograph records. In 1942 Schaeffer became the Director of Acoustic Music with Radiodiffusion Television Françaises (RTF), which gave him access to phonograph turntables, disc recording devices, a direct-disc cutting lathe, mixers, and a large library of sound effect records. He quickly discovered that he could lock-groove records, which meant that

Schaeffer and His Original Tools

Pierre Schaeffer approached audio recording from a designer's perspective. His developments, inventions, and designs were very forward-thinking. His musique concrète compositions used natural sounds structured in various ways to create interesting and pioneering recorded sounds and textures.

As modern musicians searched for new ways to create music, they turned to many of Schaeffer's developments for artistic expression and inspiration.

Schaeffer experimented with several different editing techniques in which the analog tape was cut at different angles to achieve various sonic effects. He was even known to cut tape in long horizontal segments, taping them back together in random or calculated order.

Analog Tape Editing Techniques

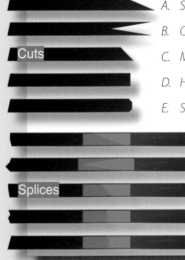

A. *Soft attack or decay*

B. *Combined attack and decay of two sounds*

C. *Medium attack or decay*

D. *Hard attack or abrupt finish*

E. *Softer and less abrupt than D*

Analog tape, edited with demagnetized razor blades, was precisely marked, cut, and connected together with adhesive tape. Adhesive editing tape evolved into a trustworthy tool that bonded the recording tape together without leaving or bleeding sticky residue. In any analog recording domain it is crucial that the head gap remain clean and free from any oxide or adhesive.

rather than continuing to spiral toward the center of the disk, the needle would stay in the same groove and repeat the same audio information. In essence, he created the first artistic use of the loop.

As the '50s saw the introduction of the first functional analog tape recorders, Schaeffer immediately incorporated them into his musical experimentations. He worked with speed changes, actual tape loops, razor-blade editing, combinations of loops, and other musical and natural sounds. He was fascinated by many of the same sound manipulations that fascinate us today.

In his attempt to give structure to his creative genre, Schaeffer divided sounds into four functional categories. With this categorization he began to try to devise a system of notation. The four categories of sounds, as described by Schaeffer, are

1. Living elements, such as voices
2. Noises
3. Prepared instruments
4. Conventional instruments

The first analog machine he used included a 5-track machine. He often used this machine as a multitrack playback device, setting two speakers in front on the left and right, one speaker directly in the back of the room, and one speaker overhead for vertical positioning of sounds. The fifth channel was used for a live microphone, which was distributed to the other speakers. This system provided a way for real-time augmentation from a performer using the handheld mic. Does this sound familiar to anyone? This is truly a predecessor to modern-day surround systems. Keep in mind that stereo sound was still in development and the analog tape recorder had just become functionally available.

Schaeffer also developed a tape recorder, called the Morpho-phone, which contained 12 playback heads, so he was able to easily experiment with changing tape delays and pseudo reverberation effects in conjunction with speed changes and timing variations between tracks.

Another machine he invented was called the Phonogene. It was designed to play prerecorded tape loops at different speeds and even came with a 12-note keyboard to trigger the playback speeds!

The Mellotron

There have been several distinct technological developments in the music world that have impacted the artistic and creative landscape, and as we've begun to see through Pierre Schaeffer's groundbreaking developments, the world of electronic music has had a very interesting history. Many of the early technological developments, which lead to the digital sampler, culminated in a keyboard called the Mellotron. Even though Schaeffer's tape-based keyboard, the Phonogene, preceded its development, so many influential musicians commercially embraced the Mellotron that its impact and importance is undeniable.

The path to the Mellotron was long and winding. These historical highlights demonstrate the musician's common desire to incorporate interesting sounds into the sonic palette.

- During the 1920s the Theremin was developed by Leon Theremin. This instrument, played by moving your hands around a metallic rod or plate, still defines the eerie sounds of sci-fi. In the 1960s the Beach Boys used the Theremin for the whistle-like sound in "Good Vibrations."

+ In the early 1930s, German scientists developed the fundamental process by which audio could be recorded onto magnetic tape. On Christmas day in 1932 the British Broadcasting Corporation first used a tape recorder for their broadcast.

+ In 1935, engineers at AEG (*Allgemeine Elektrizitäts-Gesellschaft*) in Germany, along with developers at the German chemical giant, I.G. Farben, demonstrated the first practical tape recorder. During WWII, AEG engineers discovered the AC biasing technique, which is responsible for the accurate and natural-sounding audio recording quality as we know it today. By 1943 they had developed the first stereo tape recorder.

+ In 1935 Laurens Hammond invented the tone wheel, a sound generator that eventually led to the development of the Hammond B-3 organ.

+ At the end of WWII, John T. Mullin, American audio engineer and member of the US Army Signal Corps, was part of a team instructed to find out as much as they could about German radio and electronics. In their plunder, Mullin was given two AEG Magnetophone high-fidelity recorders and 50 reels of tape. He sent them back to the US in multiple pieces, and upon his return from the war, immediately reassembled them and improved on their design.

+ In 1942 Pierre Schaeffer began using real sounds from vinyl media as loops, lock-grooved to maintain constant playback. Once analog tape was available, he developed the Morphophone, a 12-head tape recorder capable of interesting delay and reverberation effects, and the Phonogene, a series of tape loops triggered from a special 12-note to play back.

+ In 1947 John Mullin set out to convince Hollywood to adopt the analog tape recorder for commercial radio production. In June 1947, he demonstrated the magnetic tape recorder for Bing Crosby, who immediately realized its commercial and creative potential. Whereas live radio was the norm, this new tape format would let Crosby record and edit his shows in the comfort of the studio. Bing, using the same recorders and tape stock that Mullins brought home from Germany, put the first analog tape recorders into commercial use.

+ By 1948, with $50,000 in backing from Bing Crosby, a small six-man company called Ampex had developed a process to produce magnetic recording tape and had released the Model 200 analog tape recorder, which used essentially the same design as John Mullin's German Magnetophones.

+ In 1952, Harry Chamberlain of Upland, California developed a keyboard called the Chamberlain that controlled a series of eight-second analog tape segments. The keyboard typically consisted of 35 keys, each with its own tape. Using quarter-inch tape, running at 7 1/2 inches per second, the high-fidelity analog recordings offered unlimited potentially for the creative world. Eventual formats even provided multiple tracks on each tape, so with a simple switch the Chamberlain could switch between up to 16 real instrument sounds. Harry's first instrument was the Model 100 Rhythmate; it had 14 tapes of drum patterns and was aimed at the home organ market. The original tapes also included organ and string sounds.

The Mellotron Arrives

On a quest to find 70 matched recording heads, Chamberlain's salesman, Bill Fransen, found the Bradley Brothers (Lesley, Frank, and Norman) of Bradmatic, Ltd. in Birmingham, England. The Bradleys showed such interest in the Chamberlain that in 1962 Fransen returned to England with a presentation demonstrating its capabilities. The Bradleys were immediately interested in improving the design and turning the Chamberlain into a commercially viable instrument. By the end of 1962, the prototype of their version of the Chamberlain, called the Franson, was complete. Prior to commercial release the instrument name was changed to the Mellotron, and the new Bradley-owned manufacturing

The Original Mellotron

The original Mellotron and the Chamberlain were very heavy, resembling a console organ. Since they were designed with the home organ industry in mind, portability and user technical interaction were unexpected. With the immediate acceptance into the pop music genre, the Melletron eventually stream-lined its design, shed much of its weight, and adopted features that served the professional musician.

The Melletron Mark I started the phenomenon with this double 35-note keyboard model.

The Chamberlain, developed by Harry Chamberlain, preceded the Mellotron. The original Mellotron was very similar to the Chamberlain.

Lesley Bradley at the keyboard of the Mark II, with an M300 in the background and a 400 immediately behind him. Photo Credit: Mellotron Archives

entity was named Melody Electronics, and eventually Mellotronics, then finally Streetly Electronics. In 1966 the Bradley brothers bought the Mellotron technology from Harry Chamberlain for $30,000.

The initial release of the Mellotron was the Mark I. It was basically a copy of the Chamberlain Music Master and it looked much like a console organ, with a high-quality mahogany veneer finish. About 55 units were produced between 1962 and 1963. The Mark II included several design improvements. About 250 of this upgraded design were released between 1964 and 1967.

The Melletron Mechanism

The illustration below demonstrates the mechanism behind the operation of the Mellotron. Each key contains the complete mechanism in which a six-foot piece of magnetic tape is clamped at both ends (11, 12), pulled past the playback head assembly (8), and then through tension at the spring and weight mechanism (7, 8), allowed to return to its rest position. Traveling at 7 1/2 inches per second, the tape takes about eight seconds to stall with all of the slack in the bin (A, 4). When the key is pressed, the capstan (2) and pinch roller (9) pinch the tape to cause the tape motion, and the felt pad (8) presses the tape against the playback head. When the key is released, and the pinch roller moves away from the capstan, the spring (7) and weight (8) pull the slack from the bin (4) so that the slack (5) is ready to perform the process again.

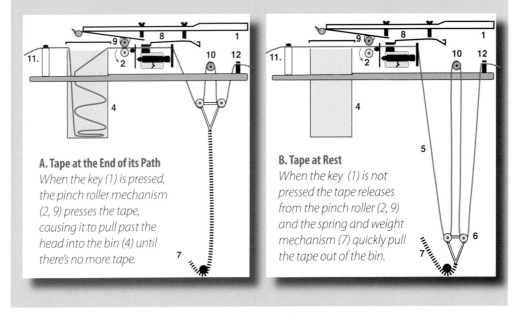

A. Tape at the End of its Path
When the key (1) is pressed, the pinch roller mechanism (2, 9) presses the tape, causing it to pull past the head into the bin (4) until there's no more tape.

B. Tape at Rest
When the key (1) is not pressed the tape releases from the pinch roller (2, 9) and the spring and weight mechanism (7) quickly pull the tape out of the bin.

Even though the number of initial Mellotrons sold might seem unimpressive, the instrument's impact on music creativity was vast. Virtually all of the influential musicians in the commercial pop music field put the Mellotron through its paces.

Mike Pinder, an employee of Streetly Electronics, tested the Mellotrons at the end of the manufacturing process to make sure they were completely functional. His love for the instrument grew and he bought one for himself and incorporated it into his new band, the Moody Blues. Pinder used the Mellotron on their hit single release, "Love and Beauty," and shortly thereafter introduced the instrument to the Beatles, who used it for the flute sounds on "Strawberry Fields Forever."

The Mellotron Model 400

The Mellotron Model 400 was a direct answer to the professional musician's needs. As a virtual feather-weight in comparison to the original Mark I and II, the 400 weighed 122 pounds. The mechanism was streamlined and tuning was re-initiated—the Model 300 didn't have tuning, which was a big problem for musicians on the road or in areas where inconsistent power caused the capstan motors to run at unpredictable speeds.

The Mellotron Model 400

Inside the Mellotron Model 400

The Mellotron became the tool of choice for many popular artists, and the Bradley brothers and Harry Chamberlain continued to build updated models that addressed consumer needs. The Model 300 and 400 became much more portable, incorporating a single 52-note keyboard and multichannel tapes. The Model 400 was the lightest Mellotron, weighing 122 pounds, and almost every major group used it in the 1970s.

In 1977, Dallas Musical Instruments of Mahwah, New Jersey (Bill Eberline) took over worldwide distribution of the Mellotron. When all was said and done, Dallas Musical Instruments (DMI) collapsed, taking Mellotronics with them. The Bradleys and Streetly Electronics barely made it through the failure of DMI intact. In fact, they ended up selling the Mellotron name to Eberline in the legal battle that ensued after DMI's demise.

A Sample List of Artists Using the Mellotron

So many artists in the US, Europe, and all around the world were very taken with the Mellotron. This was the first commercially available instrument that let the musician use real instrument sounds without actually hiring the real player.

ABBA	Genesis	Paul McCartney	Bob Seger
Aerosmith	Hall and Oats	Moody Blues	Steve Miller Band
Alice Cooper	George Harrison	Pink Floyd	Thin Lizzy
B-52s	Michael Jackson	Prince	Uriah Heep
The Beach Boys	Jethro Tull	Red Hot Chili Peppers	Suzanne Vega
The Beatles	Elton John	REM	Violent Femmes
The Bee Gees	King Crimson	The Rolling Stones	Tom Waits
Black Sabbath	Lenny Kravitz	Todd Rundgren	Ric Wakeman
David Bowie	John Lennon	Rush	Wishbone Ash
Elvis Costello	Led Zepplin	Santana	Yes
Cream	Lynyrd Skynyrd	Scorpions	

The Bradleys continued to build the Mellotron under the name of Novatron. Bill Eberline eventually ended up forming a company called Sound Sales that sold Mellotrons and tapes.

In 1987, due to the synthesizer boom of the 1980s and the development and commercial viability of digital samplers, Streetly Electronics went out of business. However, original Mellotron sounds are still available in CD-ROM format and can easily be incorporated into any sampler library, complete with the sound of the playback head touching the tape and the original recording length.

The immediate musical affinity for the Mellotron truly demonstrates the power of the demand for new sounds that has always existed in music production. The original Mellotron tapes, developed over 50 years ago, equate directly to our modern use of digital samples and loops. This important instrument helped drive the musical instrument industry to embrace modern technology as a viable business and a creative musical tool.

Compositional Techniques in the 1950s and 1960s

The Beatles' "Revolution 9" from the *White Album* used portions of symphonic recordings. In their experimental phase the Beatles used many different techniques with analog tape that were extremely creative and inventive. In fact, the rumored death of Paul McCartney sent fans scouring through their recordings in detail, uncovering many subtle techniques the Beatles used to increase the power and emotion of their music.

Random techniques, such as cutting a passage into equal lengths and then taping them back together in random order, or playing the tape backwards, or very fast, or very slow, created interesting sounds. The creative minds of history accomplished many of the sonic gymnastics that we take for granted today. Whereas we simply push a button to achieve any number of mind-blowing effects, musical pioneers had to spend hours to create a similar sound. I believe that we should strive to apply the same kind of creative thinking to our current craft of music and sound that the early pioneers did. Who knows what we might come up with!

Modern Sampling Techniques

The predecessors of modern sampling were Jamaican DJs, who developed what they called *dub*. Dub combined portions of reggae grooves with other recordings. Some of the DJs would even rap over the top of their recordings using improvised lyrics. This form eventually evolved into hip-hop.

All of these early uses of sampling were performed in the analog domain, either on tape or from a vinyl album. It wasn't until the mid-'80s that commercial samplers became sonically acceptable and commercially available at an affordable price.

The mid-'80s also saw the development of an art form called *Plunderphonics*. In this genre, like in musique concréte, essentially all ingredients of a composition are taken (plundered) from other recordings. Often the source recordings are from films, educational videos, dialogue, or sound effects, in addition to previously recorded musical compositions.

Kool DJ Herc is credited with drawing all of the previously used sampling techniques into a form that directly resulted in the true hip-hop sound. Starting in the west Bronx in New York, this musical form rapidly spread to all of New York City, and the rest is history. Hip-hop quickly became popular throughout the musical community, with many of the innovative sampling techniques and improvisational concepts spilling into other genres.

Analog Tape Loops

In the modern recording world, the drum loop repeats itself until you pick another loop. Tempos are easily changed to match the song, and pitches and even instruments are often easily interchanged. In the analog world, the loop was actually a physical loop of tape that played over and over. On the *Gaucho* album, Steely Dan used tape loops to lock in absolutely the most perfect drum groove.

Setup and manipulation of the tape loop was much more cumbersome than the way we control loops today. With analog tape the first step was to record the audio onto a 2-track recorder. Next, the desired section had to be located, carefully marked, and cut out of the reel using a razor blade. Finally, the extracted tape needed to be taped together into a loop, which could be played continuously around the tape path.

All edits had to be clean and perfectly placed. Also, keep in mind that virtually every time a loop was created, it didn't fit nicely around the tape path—there needed to be a creative extension of the tape path. Usually a mic stand would suffice, positioned outside the normal tape path just enough so that when the tape ran around it, the tape tension was sufficient to keep consistent tape-to-playback-head contact. Considering that most high-quality mixdown recorders ran at 30 inches per second, the loops could be somewhat large. Even at 120 bpm, a four-bar loop lasted about eight seconds, which resulted in a loop that was about 20 feet (240 inches) long.

Tape Delays and Loops

Tape loops and delays were used widely in the recording industry before the development and commercialization of analog and digital delays.

Tape Loops
Tape loops were constructed by editing out the segment to be looped, splicing the ends together to form a loop, and then physically designing a tape path that fit the size of the loop. Microphone stands became the tool of choice, allowing the engineer to place the necessary number of stands close to the tape machine in order to shape the path that fit the length of tape and the room.

Tape Delays
Modern digital delay devices provide control over every believable parameter, typically across multiple delays. For a simple delay, analog recorders record the incoming signal at the record head and play it back immediately from the playback head—the delay time was controlled by the tape speed and the fixed distance between the heads.

Tape loop wraps around mic stands

Erase Head   Record Head   Playback Head

Modern Digital Samplers

The very first digital samplers were cumbersome, virtually unaffordable to anyone but the recording elite, low fidelity, and at the same time revolutionary, impressively feature-laden, and immediately embraced by the recording industry.

In 1979 CMI, an Australian company, introduced the Fairlight for about $60,000—the first commercially released sampler. Around the same time, New England Digital released the Synclavier, and shortly thereafter E-MU released the Emulator. The first Emulator released in 1981 was almost affordable at $9,995, and it brought sampling capabilities to most mid-level studios of the '80s. In 1982 E-MU lowered the price to $7,995.

These original samplers were all capable of 8-bit samples, with E-MU boasting a 27.5-kHz, 8-bit process that sonically approximated a 12-bit sample! The original Fairlight was capable of 24-kHz, 8-bit recording. Even the expensive Fairlight was limited to 8-note polyphony, with the original Emulator sporting two voices and a whopping 64-kB RAM. E-MU quickly introduced 4- and 8-voice models with 128-kB RAM.

Ensoniq propelled the sampling craze by introducing the Mirage in 1986 for $1,695. This was the first affordable sampler and it really provided some impressively competitive features, such as:

+ Eight-bit samples from 5- to 15-kHz sample rate
+ 128-kB RAM
+ Eight-voice polyphony
+ Two-part multitimbral
+ Analog filters
+ Up to two oscillators per voice
+ Split keyboard
+ Sample editing
+ Eight-song, 333-note sequencer

Around the same time (1984), Akai came along with the S612, although in 1986 they introduced a new higher-resolution sampler and quickly began to dominate the feature-per-dollar race with their S-series samplers and MPC-series digital MIDI sequencer/synthe-

Early Digital Samplers

Early digital samplers were the predecessors of the modern digital audio workstation. The Fairlight, Synclavier, and Emulator I offered unprecedented control over audio. Though modern technology is far superior sonically, technically, and musically, it is incredible just how much these early devices could do.

Samplers by Emulator, Ensoniq, and Akai brought sampling technology to the masses. When these devices were new, musicians and engineers were wowed by their capabilities and immediately found creative ways to get incorporate them into their recordings.

New England Digital's Synclavier was an industry leader in progressive new sampling techniques. They decided that, since RAM was very expensive, they would devise a sample architecture that played directly off the internal 10-megabyte hard drive—the first hard disc recorder. They also established a variable sample rate on each voice from 1 kHz to 100 kHz—all 16-bit words. They led the way in stereo sampling and, when business became tough due to increased competition, they created a software-based system that carried an annual renewal fee of $5,000.

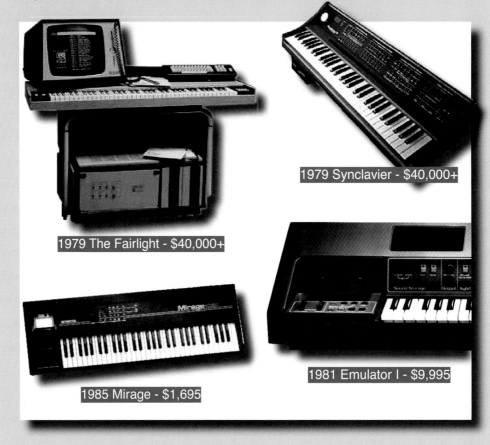

1979 Synclavier - $40,000+

1979 The Fairlight - $40,000+

1981 Emulator I - $9,995

1985 Mirage - $1,695

sizer/samplers. They raised the bar by increasing bit and sample rates, providing built-in monitor outputs for easy and efficient sample editing, and by providing a platform for an amazing number of third-party sample libraries. Eventually, the MPC4000 offered up to 24-bit, 96-kHz sampling, up to 512 MB of sampling RAM, 16 velocity-sensitive drum pads, an intuitive 64-track sequencer, and a USB port for easy connection to external drives or Macs or PCs.

Legality

The very first commercially successful hip-hop recording was released in the late '70s. In it, the Sugarhill Gang used a part the Chic's "Good Times" as the foundation for "Rapper's Delight." Along with its commercial success came the first legal problems—Bernard Edwards and Nile Rodgers, who wrote "Good Times," weren't given credit.

The early legal battles over copyright infringement and downright musical thievery were sometimes settled amicably out of court and sometimes tried furiously in drawn-out court battles.

There have been several high-profile cases in which the original artists were awarded huge settlements because of the illegal use of their recordings. Once the settlements began to fall in the favor of the original artists and composers, you might think the trends would change in the music industry; however, sampling and the use of other people's music is still an issue on occasion.

The correct and legal way to use samples of previously recorded music is to obtain authorization and clearance from the copyright holders in advance. Once the agreement is established and clearance and licensing for use have occurred, a group can be relatively—although not completely—assured that the usage will stand up in a court of law.

Sample Basic Training

H istorically, a sample could be created through the proper use and manipulation of tape or a vinyl recording. Modern samples are nothing more than digital recordings.

Whereas a sample is technically the binary quantification of the amplitude status of an analog waveform at a specific moment in time, in practice the term *sample* often refers to the entirety of a certain digital recording. For instance, a drum sample typically refers to a digital recording of a drum that has been hit once. This digital sample is often stored in memory in such a way that it be can played back in response to MIDI note data that comes from a MIDI keyboard. The MIDI keyboard and associated MIDI-controlled recorder/storage device are what make a sampler.

Sample Quality

Whereas the original Fairlight cost over $40,000 for 8-bit, 24-kHz sampling, current software samplers can be found as freeware or

Modern Samplers

Modern samplers contain virtually any imaginable parameter control. The main distinction between a sampler and any other digital workstation is the sampler's connection with a MIDI keyboard or other MIDI controller. Hardware samplers contain the capacity for large amounts of data use and storage with a built-in keyboard or a MIDI jack for connection to a MIDI controller. The software sampler resides within the DAW as a virtual instrument plug-in, which is connected to the MIDI controller via computer-controlled routing.

The software sampler below is Mark of the Unicorn's Mach Five. It provides awesome control along with a user-friendly interface. It accepts samples from virtually every sample library.

The hardware sampler below is the Korg Triton-Rack. The Triton series of samplers held dominance in the marketplace because they provided power, expandability, and a relatively simple user interface.

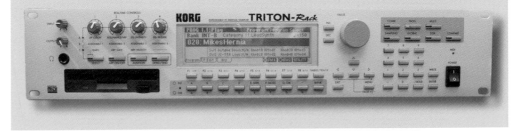

shareware that will turn your existing computer into a high-quality digital sampler. Modern hardware and software samplers should be expected to provide at least 24-bit, 96-kHz sampling. Preferably, the modern sampler should be capable of high-definition sampling at or beyond 24-bit, 192-kHz. Ideally your sampler should provide up to or beyond 32-bit, 384-kHz file support, capacity for hundreds of voices, at least 16-way multitimbral output, unlimited layers, and capacity for several different sample formats.

Sample Formats

There are several different types of sample formats. Many of the manufacturers produce proprietary formats. Most new samplers—especially software samplers—read many, if not all, of these formats, including AKAI, E-MU, Roland, Kurzweil, GIGA, Kontakt, EXS24, SF2, LM4, LM4 MkII, REX, ZeroX BeatCreator, WAV, AIF, SD II, ISO & Nero Disc Image, Toast CD-Image, MP3, and Soundfont.

In addition, samplers should provide support for popular plug-in formats, especially VST, DXi, and AU.

Technical Considerations

Learn the basic technical aspects of sampling so you understand the implications of how you use this valuable tool. Practice working with a sampler to completely understand the amazing power and creativity derived from this important technological advancement.

Sample RAM

Whether recording or importing, the first place a sample is stored is in RAM (*Random Access Memory*). This is where samples reside in performance mode so that all samples are instantly accessible with no lost time as the processor reads and transfers the sample data from its storage location.

Sampler RAM

The amount of available random access memory (RAM) in any sampler determines the amount of sample data that can be processed, performed, stored, or otherwise manipulated. As samplers have increased in capacity, multiple slots for RAM have greatly increased the sampler's processing potential.

The original samplers had a RAM capacity in the range of 64 to 128 kilobytes. Modern hardware samplers offer RAM capacities in the hundreds of megabytes. Modern software samplers utilize the computer's onboard RAM, which, even though it is shared with the OS and applications, offers potentially several gigabytes.

There is one primary delineation between a sampler and a hard disk recorder. The sampler operates from data stored in RAM; therefore, it can transpose instantaneously, such as when the root note of the sample is played over a range of keys—conceptually, each sample can be performed on multiple keys and at various pitches. The hard disk recorder operates primarily from data stored on the hard drive so certain manipulations, such pitch adjustment, must be selected and processed separately.

The only problem with RAM is that it is volatile, meaning when the power shuts off, the sample RAM dissipates—your sample data evaporates, it's lost, gone, kaput, never to be seen again until you rerecord or reload it. Through the use of RAM cards and internal powering, it's possible to make a sampler feel like the samples stick around when the unit powers down, but sample data somehow must be loaded and stored in a recallable fashion to a quick and efficient storage medium.

Adding Additional Storage

Many early samplers utilized 5.25-inch floppy disks to save and recall sample data. This seemed great at the time because nobody knew any better. However, even at the time everyone knew what slow was, and these things were slow! The more detailed the sample data, the longer the store and recall process. The following quote is straight out of the E-MU Drumulator SP-12 manual. It defines the era very well.

"Note: This [saving a full bank of samples] takes a very, very, very, very, very, long time if you have a Turbo SP-12 and the User sound memory is full. While waiting for the sounds to be saved, you have an excellent opportunity to learn a new language, become an airline pilot, or take a brief overseas vacation. And we might as well warn you now... you may need two disks to save all the sounds. If so, the display will ask you to insert Disk #2; press YES to continue the saving process. Cheer up, though; it doesn't take anywhere near as long to save the second disk as the first one. The slow operation is inherent in the 1541 drive, not the SP-12."

Most modern samplers provide some pathway to a SCSI connection, possibly as an optional add-on. With this connection or the increasingly popular inclusion of FireWire and USB connections, a hard drive can be incorporated in the system, which allows for fast access to stored data and a quick and easy place to store your custom sample data.

The only problem with these quick and easy storage devices is finding a specific sample among hundreds or thousands of others. You must be careful and deliberate in your labeling process. I've found a numbering system to be very convenient in these circumstances.

Make up a legend of your sound categories and start each category with the appropriate number. You might end up with a lot of sounds, so plan to use two digits—always lead with zeros. Instead of labeling kick drums as category 1, label them as 01. Break the categories into individual drums, types of bass guitar, acoustic pianos, electric pianos, distorted electric guitars, electric guitars, acoustic guitars, and so on. Using this system, you can describe the sounds however you want, but all sounds in the same category will always group together when sorted alphabetically.

Sample Duration and Size

It has gotten to the point where modern samplers are equipped with enough RAM to store several minutes of samples. The more RAM the device contains, the greater the available sample time. The exact amount

Basic Organizational Considerations

Whether you're keeping track of loops, samples, or synth patches, you need an organized and intelligent system. This window from Spectrasonics Stylus RMX is an excellent example of a system where each master group of grooves is given a numeric value. When the master group (Suites) is selected in the column on the left, it reveals the list of associated variations and groove ingredients in the column on the right (Elements)—each of these variations carries the same master number.

of sample time depends on the sample parameters—a 16-bit, 44.1-kHz sample takes up less space than a 24-bit, 192-kHz sample.

The formula to determine the amount RAM compared to the sample time is pretty simple—just consider what you already know from *The S.M.A.R.T Guide to Digital Recording, Software, and Plug-Ins.*

+   There are eight bits in a byte.

+ Samples are noted in samples per second.

+ There are 60 seconds in a minute.

+ Multitrack samples occupy a proportionally greater amount of space by a factor of the number of channels. Therefore, stereo samples occupy twice the space of mono samples, and 5.1 surround samples occupy six times the space of mono samples.

With all of this in mind, do the math. Multiply 16 bits by 44.1 kHz to find the number of bits per second. In this case, calculate 16 bits times 44,100 to derive 705,600 bits per second. Because there are eight bits in a byte, divide 705,600 by eight, and you will discover there are 88,200 bytes in a second.

Unfortunately, calculating from bytes to kilobytes, megabytes, gigabytes, and terabytes is not as simple as simply moving the decimal point to the left by three, six, nine, or 12. Most people simply understand that a kilobyte is a thousand bytes, a megabyte is a million bytes, a gigabyte is a billion bytes, and a terabyte is a trillion bytes. Although that provides a relatively valuable mental picture, it's not really accurate.

Digital data consists of binary data with two possible bit states: on (1) or off (0). The actual numbers of bits associated with amounts of data are based on these exponential values:

+ A byte equals 2^3 equals 8 bits

+ A kilobyte equals 2^{10} equals 1,024 bytes

+ A megabyte equals 2^{20} equals 1,048,576 bytes equals 1,024 kilobytes

+ A gigabyte equals 2^{30} equals 1,073,741,824 bytes equals 1,024 megabytes

+ A terabyte equals 2^{40} equals 1,099,511,657,776 bytes equals 1024 gigabytes

So far you have discovered that there are 88,200 bytes per second. Multiply that by 60 to get 5,292,000 bytes per minute. Divide that by 1,048,576 to find that a mono minute of CD-quality audio occupies about 5.05 megabytes.

If you're using stereo samples, simply double the space required per mono minute of CD-quality audio to obtain about 10.1 megabytes.

Compare the previous calculations to a stereo 24-bit, 192-kHz sample.

+ 24 bits x 192 kHz x 2 = 9,220,800 bits per second

+ 9,220,800 ÷ 8 bits per byte = 1,152,600 bytes per second

+ 1,152,600 x 60 seconds per minute = 69,156,000 bytes per minute of 24-bit, 192-kHz stereo audio

+ 69,156,000 ÷ 1,048,576 bytes per megabyte = 65.9 megabytes per stereo minute of 24-bit, 192-kHz audio

With all these calculations it should be easy to see that a sampler with 512 megabytes of sample RAM could hold about 100 minutes of CD-quality audio or just under eight minutes of high-definition 24-bit, 192-kHz audio.

Calculating Sample Size

Calculating the amount space needed to store a digital recording, sample, or loop involves simple math. The following formulas break down the ingredients and calculations for sample size in megabytes per minute versus megabytes per second. These calculations take into consideration the bit depth, sample rate, number of channels, and sample length.

Calculating Space Requirements for Audio Sample - Megabytes per Minute

Bits (B) x Sample Rate (SR) ÷ 8 (bits/byte) x Number of Channels (C) x 60 (seconds/min) ÷ 1,048,576 (bytes/megabyte) x Sample Length (in minutes) (M) = Megabytes

Calculating Space Requirements for Audio Sample - Megabytes per Second

This formula calculates the sample size in seconds (S) rather than minutes (M).

B x SR ÷ 8 x C ÷ 1,048,576 x (S) = Megabytes

So, for a 16-bit, 88.1-kHz surround sample that's seven minutes long, simply plug the variables into the simple equation.

16 x 88100 ÷ 8 x 6 x 60 ÷ 1,048,576 x 7 = 423.45 megabytes

Justification for Capturing High-Definition Samples

There are projects or songs that simply scream out to be recorded at the very highest audio quality, whether in the digital or analog domain. Yet any project that eventually (and only) ends up on CD is going to be converted to 16-bit, 44.1-kHz.

Project Resolution

If you're multitracking in the digital domain, and if you're recording your samples digitally to the multitrack, the sampler settings need to match the multitrack audio resolution settings. It's often a good idea to record your sampler audio at the highest reasonable resolution, and then patch into the digital multitrack via analog connections. If you prefer, convert the samples and save them as a new lower-resolution version before you record them digitally. Using this approach, you keep the best sample data you can justify, and the project still receives high-quality audio.

Final Mix Format

You need to determine what the final audio resolution will be for the project, and then you must consider whether you expect to use your samples or recordings on future projects. If you're mixing to analog tape, use the highest possible resolution audio. When the digital audio is finally mixed to analog tape, you will hear noticeable sonic improvement from higher-resolution data.

If you're mixing digitally and your project will eventually end up on CD, consider selecting 24-bit, 88.2-kHz or 24-bit, 176.4-kHz sample rates because the whole-number multiples of 44.1 kHz down-convert to CD-quality audio more accurately.

Modern samplers have become so powerful that the sampler itself might act as the instrument and the mixdown platform. With this in mind, the line blurs between sampler resolution and multitrack resolution—they might be the same.

Commercially Released Format

If the final released format will be CD only, it's hard to justify committing to HD audio. However, recordings are frequently released in multiple formats—be prepared for the best. If there's any chance that your music will be released in 5.1 DVD Audio, SACD, or another high-resolution format, you will be very disappointed if you haven't made the extra effort to record HD audio.

Potential Historical Value

You might not think that the music you're working on has great historical value. However, it only takes one uncomfortable incident to demonstrate the folly of that type of thinking. You never know when something good will happen for the project you're recording today. I have personally experienced the humiliation of erasing the wrong reel of tape and of cutting corners on the wrong song—it doesn't feel good and it doesn't make anyone look good around you.

Always hold your standards high. In fact, hold them as high as humanly possible. No one will ever give you anything but praise for warranting their music important enough to nitpick. The truly great get to be great by expecting greatness and putting forth a truly great effort in the interest of greatness.

Processor Speed and Drive Capacity

The fact is, HD audio is demanding on the audio processor and it is a data-space hog. If you want to record much HD audio, you need a very fast processor. If you're recording several tracks and you want to use plug-ins, such as effects and dynamics processors, you might need multiple processors working together to perform the task.

Every time I buy a new computer for music I feel like I can do anything—the sky's the limit. Then, after a couple weeks of discovering the cool new things I never could have done with the previous computer, I reach that sad point when I've figured out how to overtax the new computer. Thankfully, processor sharing and distribution is becoming more common, so you can install another new computer to take up the slack.

The bottom line is, you can only do what you can do. The disadvantage to overtaxing your processor is that the computer or sampler is forced to sacrifice something. If you're playing back several HD tracks with plug-ins, the computer might seem to keep up with the process but the groove might start to feel odd. Your device is trying to get the data to flow as accurately as possible, but there is a point when it just can't keep up.

Typically, the measure counter is one of the least important features. If your sampler or computer is playing audio and the measure counter is pausing and running erratically, you can see that there are attempts being made to process the important information. When this starts to happen, close your eyes and listen to the music. If you think something doesn't feel quite right with the groove, you're probably right. At this point, start to thin things out a bit. Turn off some effects, consolidate some tracks, close some windows, or even take a break and let everything cool down.

Sometimes RAM becomes glitchy because data has been going in and out over and over and over. It might help to simply power down for a minute to let the stored memory dissipate. Often, drives become fragmented because data is constantly being written and erased and written again. Simply defragmenting your storage drives can make your device feel like a brand-new hot rod.

Hardware versus Software Samplers

Software samplers are much less expensive than hardware samplers. They're more powerful, easier to edit with, easier to organize sounds with, capable of using virtually any sample format, able to manipulate HD audio samples with ease, and they are constantly upgraded with new features and capabilities—stuff you haven't yet learned that you can't live without. You might think, "Why even bother? I'll just spend a couple hundred bucks on a software sampler and get on with it." Ah, not so fast, grasshopper. Carefully consider the pathway on which you walk.

Hardware Sampler Strengths

Hardware samplers offer several strengths and advantages over software samplers. Their effectiveness and convenience is very dependent on the intended application. In a live setting the hardware sampler is very powerful. In a recording environment, hardware samplers are useful and efficient, but in general software samplers provide greater power and flexibility.

Shared Processing

Adding the processing power of a modern sampler to a recording setup is a bonus. Rather than draining the processing power of your computer with sampler tasks, you can free up power to use more plug-ins, record more tracks, or just run more consistently and stably.

The sound quality will often be as good with your sampler as with your software-based recording system. Keep your OS current so your sampler is performing to its optimum capacity at all times.

Even though your sampler has a keyboard, which is mapped to several samples, the sequencing software can still handle all of the MIDI data. It's usually more trouble than it's worth to sync the MTC clock in your DAW with the MTC clock in the sampler for most applications. It's very simple to trigger the samples from your MIDI controller through the DAW.

On the other hand, if you want to include effects from your sampler that need to occur in sync with your DAW, you will definitely need to set the sampler to follow the DAW MTC clock. Additionally, any time you want to record digitally from the sampler into your DAW, you must set the sampler to lock to the DAW word clock, or the DAW to lock to the sampler clock, or both to lock to the same external word clock source.

Simple Word Clock Connections

To get the most out of your digital samples, you should transfer them digitally whenever possible. Anytime digital data is transferred between two digital devices, there must be some kind of word clock connection. When digital connections are made, one device becomes the master. The master sets the word clock rate that will be followed, sample for sample, by other connected devices (slaves) that are set to follow the word clock.

Depending on the complexity of your system, a central word clock generator might be a necessity. If you want your system to work together in the utmost efficiency, use a highly respected word clock generator, which generates all forms of audio and video word clock, SMPTE time code, MTC. Sony 9-pin, and ADAT sync. Devices like the Apogee Big Ben and the MOTU Video Timpiece do a great job of providing simultaneous synchronization data to multiple devices at the same time.

Hardware Sampler: Digital Output to Digital Input

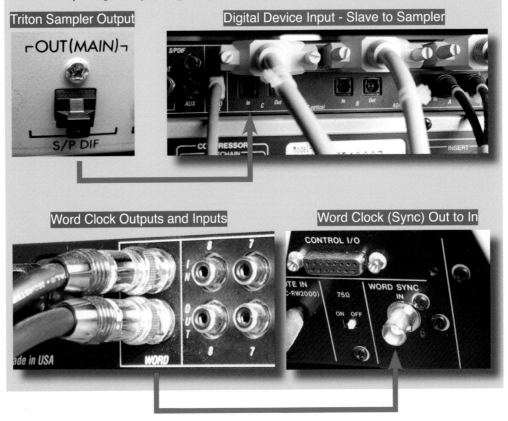

Compatibility with Live Performance Environment

Once you become proficient with a hardware sampler operating system, it becomes clear that there is efficiency in sampling with a tool designed specifically for the task at hand. The integration of the technical process with built-in performance features streamlines the transition from the source to the stage.

Sometimes, live samples are captured during a performance and immediately put to work supporting the show. Because the sample records directly into the hardware sampler, where it can be edited easily and quickly for immediate incorporation, the hardware sampler adds power and many creative options to any live performance.

The software sampler is also powerful in a live show, but even though a computer-based user interface is extremely capable of quick and complex edits, it adds another set of steps to the sampling process, which creates potential for decreased efficiency.

Creative Freedom

Comparing the creative freedom offered by hardware- and software-based samplers involves considering a few different factors.

+ Is the sampler used in a live or studio production?

+ Does the artist work in great detail or very quickly?

+ Are the samples being recorded or just played back and manipulated?

+ Are there many effects required?

+ How large is the sample library?

+ How much time is allotted for setup and striking?

It's interesting to compare hardware- and software-based samplers. Both have a computer as a brain—the hardware sample simply houses the computer and utilizes a proprietary operating system. They both use a keyboard or other MIDI triggering device to trigger the samples, and they're both common in the live and studio worlds.

The hardware sampler provides speed along with efficiency in performing basic editing functions. For a performance situation or time-sensitive rehearsals, the hardware system excels. In addition, when the task involves playing previously-recorded samples, the hardware sampler is the right choice. In a live setting, make up performance banks containing all the samples used in the performance (in show order), and then simply scroll through the banks during the gig. In a studio setting, structure the song, load the necessary samples into the appropriate banks, and mark the chart for each new sound with its bank and patch number.

Adding or changing effects on the hardware sampler typically involves scrolling through a maze of windows to find the appropriate effect location, then scrolling through a list of potential effects, then scrolling through more windows to adjust the effect parameters. This is often cumbersome even when you're very familiar with the various pathways. Often, the sheer inefficiency of this system compels the user to settle for a sound that is less than perfect. Once you find the right effect, save the patch under a different name. This way, the original sample and its effect remain intact for other situations, while the new version is instantly ready for the next performance.

Most hardware and software samplers provide for organization and grouping of samples into banks for quicker access; however, large sample libraries are typically cumbersome to access from the hardware sampler. The small screen and maze-like road map are not well suited to quickly finding and loading one sample among thousands. Nothing slows down the creative process like waiting for the keyboardist to scroll randomly through a huge list. If you find yourself in this situation, save any potential sound to a separate bank. This lets you quickly compare all the possibilities without scrolling back through the list. This process also makes it easier to layer two or three sounds that, although they're not perfect alone, might be perfect when layered and blended properly.

If you're in a situation where quick setup and striking are required (or at least greatly desired), the hardware sampler is the way to go. Patch into the house mixer, connect to AC power, and you're ready. The computer-based system probably requires a MIDI interface to connect to the controller keyboard, the computer must boot, the software must load, in a digital setting it might be necessary for word-clock connections, everything must communicate perfectly, and the sound gods must show you great favor—sometimes you win, sometimes you lose.

Software Sampler

If detailed sampling tasks are required in an atmosphere involving sonic perfectionism, complex effects, and high-definition audio, the software sampler excels. Computer-based software is very visual—you can see large groups of information quickly, and almost instantly you can zoom in to redraw the tiniest of waveform glitches. Looping, trimming, copying, pasting, crossfading, and so on are all very simple acts to perform. Adding effects is a simple matter, and you typically have access to all the plug-ins you use in your digital recording software.

If you are using several high-quality samples and effects, there is a potential drain on your CPU. This drain might limit the number of tracks you can record and play back or the number of possible real-time effects plug-ins. Additionally, it might make playback erratic or your CPU prone to crashes.

Compare Hardware and Software Sampler Screen

The primary advantage held by the software sampler over the hardware sampler is its clear, concise, and efficient user interface. The following items compare the number of steps from audio input to a completed sample recording. The drama of this comparison increases when editing and processing are included.

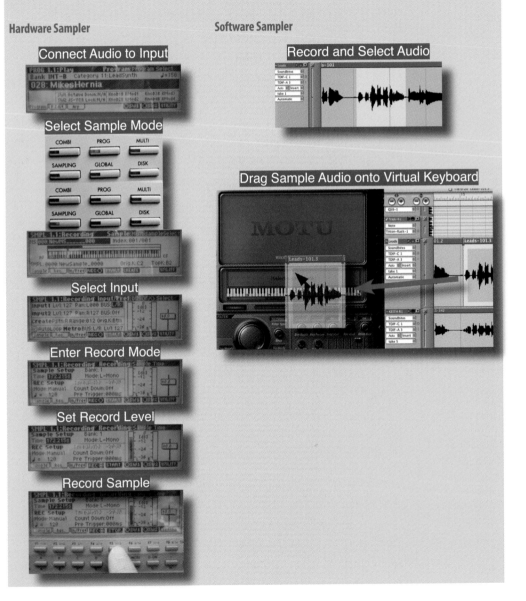

Hardware Sampler

Connect Audio to Input

Select Sample Mode

Select Input

Enter Record Mode

Set Record Level

Record Sample

Software Sampler

Record and Select Audio

Drag Sample Audio onto Virtual Keyboard

Video Example 2-1

Complicated Sampling Procedure on the Hardware Sampler

If you plan on intense sample use and demanding digital recording and playback, buy the fastest computer you can possibly afford and fill it up with RAM. With the right computer, your system will perform well and provide ample power to sample and record an impressively huge amount of information.

Software Sampler Strengths

I'm a big fan of software-based samplers. I appreciate the power and efficiency they offer in the recording environment and don't see many disadvantages in using them in a recording or live situation.

Editing

By far, the software sampler provides the most efficient means of editing, looping, and applying effects to samples. Some hardware samplers actually provide a video monitor output, which gives them some of the visual power provided by computer-based systems.

It's interesting to compare hardware and software samplers because they all include the same basic ingredients: a processor, a MIDI keyboard, a storage device, and a user interface. However, the elegance, expandability, and ease-of-use provided by the computer-based system is unmatched in the hardware realm.

Even from the very first sampling keyboard, recording a sample has never been a problem—it has always been as easy as pressing record and activating the sound source. The task that has always been most cumbersome is editing the recorded sample: cutting, copying, pasting, distributing samples across the MIDI keyboard, expanding and compressing the sample length, looping a single wave (or group of waves) to create a long tone from a short tone, and so on.

The first sampler I really used in a professional environment was the Emulator I. It held very little audio (about 17 seconds). In addition, it used a slow 5.25" floppy drive and a cumbersome user interface. The only up side compared to modern samplers was that it didn't do much with the samples; therefore, the maze of buttons and pages wasn't nearly as vast as it would have been if it performed the myriad tasks expected on today's samplers. Actually, with all things considered, it really didn't sound bad (as I recall), and I got to be pretty efficient at making it do whatever I needed it to do.

You will get to be proficient at whatever system you use, if you use it enough. The beauty of the computer-based sampling software is that it is so user friendly and so amazingly powerful that you are afforded the opportunity to quickly perform complex audio sample manipulations with impressive accuracy. Once you're proficient with this tool, your creativity is released—it is unbridled by cumbersome and confusing procedures.

Updates

Modern hardware samplers use an operating system the same way as a Mac or PC does. Occasionally, the hardware manufacturer releases an update to increase the sampler's power, eliminate bugs, or streamline some functions. However, software samplers are often updated—manufacturers frequently provide new features, a new look and feel, or a list of options you didn't know you couldn't live without. Almost every time I receive these updates, I realize—typically in the very first usage—that the day's session just wouldn't have been possible without the newest feature. Maybe I'm just a sucker for new toys.

With a computer-based system you not only receive the benefit of software updates a couple times a year, but you also get computer OS upgrades. As a Mac guy, I can't imagine going back to an early '80s operating system—it would seem limiting and powerless. The same goes for PC users. Besides, most of the new software simply couldn't run under old operating systems. When the computer OS offers new features and capabilities, software manufacturers almost immediately incorporate those features into their packages. All of this adds up to frequent and very exciting increases in the power and capacity of your sampling software.

Storage

One of the first things I bought for my Korg Triton-Rack, which I purchased in 2000, was the SCSI interface. This let me connect any SCSI drive, enabling a massive increase in the speed and efficiency of sample storage and retrieval. It worked pretty well, but the fact that everything was accessed through one small monochromatic window on the front face of this two-rack space device was a bit of a downer. Although I had a decent amount of storage space, when I compared the user interface to what I was used to on my Mac, I soon lost interest in becoming a super power user of the Triton SCSI interface. In contrast, modern sampling software, such as Mach 5 from MOTU, Kontakt from Native Instruments, HALion from Steinberg, or even IK Multimedia's Sampletank, provide easy access to all samples and a simple storage and recall procedure.

Once you start to build a sample library, you'll soon find that samples can fill up a drive quickly. With the ease and affordability of integrating FireWire and external and internal drives in the computer domain, storage space and access are not currently concerns.

Archiving samples is easily accomplished through CD-R and DVD±R. If your drives are getting full, your computer's performance will probably decrease. You should typically leave about 10 percent of your drive space empty for the OS to access the drive for its functionality, as well as for software use during normal operations. Once you reach this threshold, it's time to archive some files.

SCSI Connection

Modern hardware samplers provide a means to incorporate additional storage devices. This SCSI connection on the back of the Korg Triton-Rack allows for connections of SCSI hard drives, jazz drives, zip drives, and so on. Simply connect a large SCSI drive and access all the samples you could possibly use.

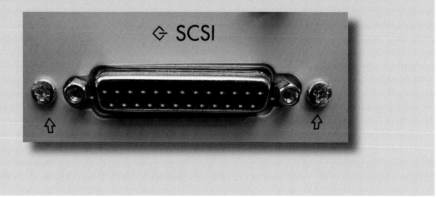

When you're finished with an album or other project, archive everything associated with that project, including all sound files, plug-in patches, software files, and any external samples used in the production. If you've incorporated several custom samples associated with a software sampler, archive those along with your other files. When you're building the samples for each production, save them in folders labeled with a reference to the project.

Processor Upgrades

I've been through several computer upgrades since computers became indispensable in the recording world. At the end of each computer's life, I felt like my productivity was decreasing rapidly. I was spending much of my time waiting for my computer to catch up, the OS crashed more frequently than usual, and my software just seemed glitchy and unpredictable. However, as soon as I received the new computer and got all the software installed, I felt like I could do anything! I couldn't believe I tolerated the old-school technology (usually a couple years old) now tucked away in a back room.

The quantum leaps in productivity, realized by incorporating the newest and fastest computer on the block, are exciting and inspiring, but at the same time it is merely the beginning of the end. Considering the rate of change in this industry, count on going through the same process in the next few years.

Hardware samplers are not likely to offer processor upgrades. Hardware OS upgrades are most likely to address bug fixes and basic operational upgrades—they're probably not going to radically affect power and functionality. Count on the hardware sampler performing about the same in five years as it does today. Count on your software

Archiving a Project for Easiest Recall

Save all of the ingredients for each project in a special folder that accompanies the project folder. Store this extra folder in the project so that no matter where or how the data is saved, duplicated, or archived, all pertinent files will be easy to find.

Save custom samples, synth patches, lyrics, PDFs of chord charts, extra audio files, pre-mastered mixes, mastered mixes, mixer documentation, album credits, and anything else that pertains directly to the musical, technical, or business aspect of the specific project.

sampler to offer a completely new and more powerful sampling experience in five years.

Compatibility with Live Performance Environment

In many ways, the hardware sampler is better suited to the live performance application than the software sampler. The simplicity of storing banks and then scrolling through patches in performance order is very

Hardware and Software Setups

This illustration demonstrates the contrasting complexities between hardware- and software-based sampler setup procedures in a live performance application.

appealing. That doesn't mean you can't or shouldn't use a software sampler in a live performance application—many great players do.

If you use a software sampler, you will be able to get to everything you need. With a little practice, you'll be able to quickly access all of your samples. Typically, a MIDI keyboard is required to play the samples. This creates the need for a MIDI interface. It also increases your setup and striking time, as well as the possibility of complications during either setup or the actual performance.

Very large shows usually incorporate software samplers along with digital recording software. Keep in mind that the top-level productions run multiple digital systems in sync throughout the show just in case something goes wrong—crashes happen. In the event of a freeze or crash, the other system takes over and the show goes on.

Even when your system is very stable, each new location or venue provides an opportunity for inconsistent and noisy power, either of which could bring down your computer-based system. With these problems, even the hardware-based system could crash, but recovery time is typically minimal compared to the time it takes to restart your computer and the applications.

Creative Freedom

In actuality, the real power of the software-based sampler lies in its ability to manipulate sampled audio—you can create truly awesome sounds very quickly. The efficient user interface provided by most software samplers, along with easy storage and editing, make software samplers fundamentally more creatively freeing than hardware-based systems. In defense of hardware samplers, they do offer great portability and simplicity in setup. In many contexts the software sampler is limiting in that, depending on your system, it isn't portable. If your computer system is bulky and designed for permanent installation, it will be difficult to accomplish off-site field recordings using the software sampler.

With all of that said, you will probably adapt well to whatever system you learn. They both offer many strengths and some weaknesses.

Building Your Own Library

There's a certain point when stock sample libraries become inadequate for your creativity. If you really focus on what sound matches your audio needs, and if that need is unique and truly special, consider building your own sample library. Build sounds that absolutely fill your needs. One of the major differences between amateur audio and high-quality professional audio is relentless attention to creative details.

Imagine What You Want

Take a step back from the project, close your eyes, and create a visual image for your musical or audio situation. Almost all sound automatically stimulates a mental image—tap into that creative reservoir. Given the opportunity, the visual image should draw you into the perfectly appropriate sonic image.

Be picky, pensive, and persistent. Music and audio are what you love or you wouldn't be reading this book, so care deeply about them. The more care you take in this craft, the better you'll be at it. Better projects will come your way, and soon you'll be working with other picky people who push you to be even more relentless and particular.

Find It

Once you see the visual image in your creative mind's eye, you'll probably be drawn to a type of sound that really fits the music you're building, the visuals you're supporting, or the story you're building. Waiting to find the perfect visual image is a much more efficient and artistically creative way to approach audio than the "poke and hope" process—the normal inclination for beginning recordists. If you find yourself aimlessly looking for a sound to inspire your creative soul, move on to another task. Most modern devices contain so many sounds and have so much sonic control that you could easily waste hours on a dead-end street.

Imagine that you're working on a heavy guitar-driven rock album and the song is very driving and punchy with a lot of tight punches and open space. The song title is "Stranglehold."

This one's pretty easy. Imagine everything around the image created by the title and combine that with the fact that the instrumentation is powerful, with nice, violent punches, kicks, and aggression. You could quickly come up with a list of images that fit this song before you even hear it. Once you hear the tight punches and violent, aggressive performance from the entire band, along with angry, screaming vocals, you can refine the visuals in your imagination. Finally, when you've had a chance to internalize the lyrics and find out that the song is about a relationship that's gone awry and both sides want more than anything to get away from a destructive and potentially dangerous situation, the vision is complete.

Make a quick list of all the imagery that comes to mind. Start fast and don't hold back. There's plenty of time to get specific, and you can always weed out ideas that seem inappropriate or downright cheesy. Your list might include

- Screams
- A fist hitting a bag of flour
- A baseball bat hitting a wooden pole
- An angry male yell
- A female shouting "No way!"
- A referee blowing a whistle

- A door being punched
- A pillow hitting a mattress very aggressively
- A hand slapping a face (or other less sensitive flesh)
- Chains dragging across pavement
- Footsteps running away
- A car horn
- A motorcycle starting and driving away
- Sounds of solitude
- A whisper
- Chanting and very disturbed voices
- Grunts
- A whimper
- A slamming door
- Television static
- Keys rattling
- A door opening

After you construct a list of images that come immediately to mind, review the list and cross out anything that is blatantly pedestrian in character or just too obvious, but keep these sounds on the list so you can evaluate them again when you're further into the sound-shaping process. They might eventually inspire you to new territory in the event of a creative dry spell.

Each item on your list is worthy of consideration because it authentically came to mind when you considered the artistic ingredients. In addition, each item should be viewed as a category to which a long list of subheading descriptions could be attributed. Avoid obvious and trite sonic inference; however, each obvious image could be your inspiration for the deeper, more metaphorical image that might provide a creative depth that is unique and enticing.

From the previous sample list, consider the few images that stick out as most powerful in relation to this song: whispers; television static and the test tone you might find in the middle of a long, painful, and uncomfortable evening; an angry male yell; and keys rattling.

One simple technique for creating custom samples uses existing sounds layered with well-crafted samples. In this instance you could sample a series of whispers and layer them over an existing synth pad or effect. Often the sampled sound creates a subliminal impact in which the sound that is recognizable and typical feels weird or delivers

Layering Samples to Create Emotion-Filled Audio

This screenshot from Native Instrument's Kontakt 2 illustrates a single sound that is made up of several ingredients. Many of the most impressive sounds are a result of layered samples such as this. Notice that in this combination there are some musical sounds and some sound effects. Each ingredient must be blended and panned for the perfect effect.

an unexpected emotion. The listener might not even be aware that there's a little something different going on emotionally, but his or her subconscious mind might recognize an emotion that is powerful and compelling.

Video Example 2-2

Layering Samples to Create Emotion

The image of television static, late nights, color bars, and an off-air test tone, along with sleeplessness and anguish, seems powerful. Try combining a slap with television static, a groan, a test tone, and a tambourine. These are ingredients that you might not have considered if you hadn't previously developed a list of creatively guided images.

Create It

When you're creating inspired samples, your quest is given direction, focus, and tangible creative momentum. There is nothing more daunting than possessing enough tools to create virtually any possible sound, yet lacking vision and direction.

Use your imagination and the previously described process to guide your sound shaping, and then go for it. Don't hold back. The creative process intimidates many people—they freeze up and can't make a move for fear that it won't be correct or good enough. If you find yourself in this predicament, take action. At a certain point, just start moving. Even if you create something unsatisfactory, at least you'll have a starting point. The process of creating sound, music, lyrics, poems, and so on should flow from your innermost being, so open up and let your creativity flow. Get your ideas out in the open and later evaluate whether they're worthy. Sometimes it's best to reveal an idea just to get it out of the way and to open the playing field for true brilliance.

Create now, evaluate later. Once you have your ideas written down, recorded, and combined, be very discerning and hard to please. Does the sound have emotional impact? Does it make you feel the way the lyrics and orchestration made you feel? Is it just right or only almost right? If it feels great and emotionally fits the song, let it be. Don't talk yourself out of a good creation. You'll build more confidence as you create sounds and emotionally lock into this creative process.

Ambience and Effects

Any time you're sampling real sounds, you must consider in the process the role of natural ambience and effects such as reverberation, delays, dynamics, and modulation. A simple sound effect might sound small and lonely by itself. On the other hand, given the right treatment, the same small sound might evolve into a giant.

As you build your sample library, include effects in your imaging considerations. If you want a gunshot to layer over a kick drum, imagine the surrounding audio space. A gunshot recorded outdoors with one microphone typically sounds like a small pop. On the other hand, when recorded with several microphones that are panned, dynamically compressed, and electronically reverberated, the sonic impact is undeniably huge!

As you've seen previously in the *S.M.A.R.T. Guide* series, compression and limiting, while limiting the loudest sounds in relation to a user-set threshold, effectively help a sound maintain a tighter dynamic space by also increasing the audibility of the softer sounds. In your study of mastering plug-ins, you've seen that the bottom-line result of limiting is actually to enable the entire mix to be boosted in level after the peak limiting process—you can make a mix sound louder.

As you build your samples, part of the polishing process involves intelligent application of compression and limiting. Whether you're recording instrumental samples, vocal sounds, or animal sounds, the compression process provides access to the components of the sound that provide an intimate and up-close aural impression.

Audio Example 2-1

The Resulting Effect of Compression

Combine Sounds

Whereas it's a good idea to layer your own custom samples over existing synthesizer sounds and samples to provide emotional impact that is unique and specific to one creative application, consider layering supportive custom samples recorded with emotional power in mind.

Sound design for film and video is the perfect application for this type of procedure. It's common for animal sounds, such as a lion's roar, to be layered with other musical sounds to increase urgency or primal fear. Other very impressionistic sounds are used to build the emotional effect of onscreen images. We've all heard these sounds and often we don't know they're even there or why they fit so well, but we're certain that they're perfect.

These sounds are the result of creative minds matching an image with a sonic impression. They are seldom the result of simply scrolling through sample banks to find a stock sound that seems to fit. Open your mind and make a list of sounds that fit the image. Build them, layer them, and enjoy them.

Your Chance to Get the Best Sounds

Sampling lets you get the very best sounds possible for your application. In addition, if you organize your library properly, over the course of a few years you will come to own a unique set of sounds that no one else uses. Therefore, your audio will develop a personality that stands out in the crowd.

Organizing the Sound Library

You might build the best sample library in the world, but if you can't find the sounds quickly and easily, they'll cause you constant frustration.

Keep Original Samples

Even though your creative process might include building effects in combination with the original sample, always save your original, dry samples separately. Typically, effects are driven by a specific emotional need. If you only save the effected sounds, you might miss the opportunity to reuse the original sample in a completely different image. Organize your samples into numbered categories, as previously mentioned, providing consistent tags to indicate versions of the sample, such as dry, fx1, fx2, and so on.

Your list of samples might include snare drums under the numbered category 002. Your actual list might include

+ 02_SNARE01_DRY
+ 02_SNARE01_FX1
+ 02_SNARE01_FX2

This way, it's obvious these sounds are all derived from the same basic snare drum sample. The degree of specificity in the sample description is up to you. This labeling decision depends on the number of characters available in your sample display. If you need to abbreviate, keep a log of your abbreviations in case you forget what in the world you were talking about over the course of years. With an intelligent abbreviation scheme, it makes more sense to include more specific labels, such as:

- 02_SNR01_dry_orig
- 02_SNR01_cmp_vrb
- 02_SNR01_lim_dly

Suggested Numbers and Abbreviations

Many standard abbreviations for orchestral instruments are based on the Latin translations. Some of the suggestions in the following list have been adjusted so they're more descriptive and obvious to the English-speaking world. Keep your list along with category numbers to enable quick and easy sorting that keeps samples together in instrument groups, no matter what you name them. For example, start all percussion sounds with the number 10 and an underscore, then use the abbreviation followed by a numeric identifier if there are multiple samples of the same type of instrument, then the sample format.

01. kick drum - kick
02. snare drum - sn
03. toms - tom
04. cymbals - cym
05. overhead mics - oh
06. hi-hats - hat
07. crash cymbal - crsh
08. ride cymbal - ride
09. splash cymbal - spl
10. percussion - perc
    - clavés - clv
    - tambourine - tamb
    - stick - stk
    - slap stick - slp stk
    - guiro - gruir

    – cabasa - cbz

    – shaker - shkr

    – maracas - mrc

    – timpani - timp

    – bongo - bon

    – quinto - con

    – conga - con

    – tumbadora- con

11. guitar - gtr

    – acoustic guitar - ac gtr

    – electric guitar - elec gtr

    – mandolin - mand

    – dobro - dbr

    – ukulele - uk

12. piano - pno

    – electric piano - elec pno

    – Fender Rhodes piano - rhds

    – clavinet - clav

    – Hammond B3 organ - B3

    – synthesizer - synth

    – full string/vocal pad - pad

13. bass guitar - bs gtr

    – acoustic bass guitar - ac bs

    – fretless bass guitar - ftls

14. brass - brs

    – trumpet - trp

    – coronet - crt

    – trombone - trb

    – tuba - tba

    – French horn - f hrn

15. saxophone - sax
    - sopranino saxophone - sno sax
    - soprano saxophone - sop sax
    - alto saxophone - alto sax
    - tenor saxophone - tn sax
    - baritone saxophone - bari sax

16. strings - str
    - violin - vl
    - viola - vla
    - cello - vlc
    - double bass - cb

17. woodwinds
    - oboe - ob
    - flute - fl
    - piccolo - picc
    - clarinet - cl
    - bass clarinet - bs cl
    - bassoon - fag

18. vocals - voc
    - backing vocals - bgv
    - soprano, alto, tenor, bass vocals - SATB
    - lead vocal - ld voc
    - vocal percussion - voc perc
    - narration - narr
    - voiceover - vo

19. effects - fx
    - dry - dry
    - compression - cmp
    - limiting - lim
    - reverberation - vrb
    - delay - dly
    - chorus - chrs
    - flanger - flng

- stereo - st
- surround sound - surr
- plate reverb - plt vrb
- echo chamber - chmb
- ambience - amb

It's also a good idea to reference the type of microphone used to record the sample. If you get used to keeping a running log that specifies any relevant details regarding the sample process, it will come to be

Examples of Abbreviation Usage

Keep your sample lists in order by adopting a consistent abbreviation format and numbering scheme. Virtually every computer-based system allows multiple sort criteria. If you always start sample titles with a number that indicates the sample family, the sample instrument, and a describer, they'll sort in a very convenient and efficient manner.

The following sample titles appear in random order in the list on the left. On the right, the list is sorted by number and instrument. It's very convenient to build a list in random order, picking and choosing whatever meets your needs. Once it is time to store the samples for future use, simply sort the list and your sounds will fall into a very user-friendly list.

Topic	Topic
11_AC_GTR_GIBSONCL40	01_KICK_22X22
04_RIDE_22"	01_KICK_29X18"
18_VOC_PERC_GRV01	01_KICK_WOOD_BTR
04_RIDE_BELL_19"	02_SN_14X6
01_KICK_29X18"	02_SN_MARCH
02_SN_14X6	02_SN_METAL_STICK
02_SN_MARCH	02_SN_MPL_TAYE
02_SN_MPL_TAYE	02_SN_WOOD_DW
11_ELEC_GTR_LES	04_CRSH_16"
04_SPL_10"	04_RIDE_20"
11_AC_GTR_TAYLOR814	04_RIDE_22"
01_KICK_22X22	04_RIDE_BELL_19"
11_AC_GTR_PRS	04_SPL_10"
04_RIDE_20"	11_AC_GTR_GIBSONCL40
11_ELC_GTR_CHRS	11_AC_GTR_PRS
14_TRP_SECTION	11_AC_GTR_TAYLOR814
01_KICK_WOOD_BTR	11_ELC_GTR_CHRS
14_TRP_HARMON	11_ELEC_GTR_LES
02_SN_WOOD_DW	11_ELEC_GTR_STRAT
18_VOC_BGV_UNISON	14_TRP_HARMON
04_CRSH_16"	14_TRP_SECTION
11_ELEC_GTR_STRAT	18_VOC_BGV_UNISON
02_SN_METAL_STICK	18_VOC_PERC_GRV01

second nature. You will never be sorry when you keep detailed information—you'll always have it just in case you need it. On the other hand, if you don't keep any records of your sampling procedure, it will be more difficult to learn from previous experiences as you continue to build your custom sample library.

Refer to http://www.billgibsonmusic.com to download an Excel list form that has proven to be an excellent tool for organizing and keeping track of samples. Click on the S.M.A.R.T. Guide Support link button to access this and other documents designed to enhance the *S.M.A.R.T. Guide* series.

Sampling

There are specific concerns that are unique to sampling, even though it is essentially identical to any digital recording process. Preparing the samples to be triggered from a MIDI device requires that the sounds be trimmed at both ends. Within the sampler your custom sounds can be layered and processed in the same way as any other keyboard sounds.

There is one excellent byproduct of recording, shaping, and preparing your own custom samples: attention to detail. For many new recordists there are so many new concepts in the recording process that many tasks get overlooked or glossed over. There's simply too much going on for many struggling enthusiasts to grasp at once. A typical sampling task focuses on one sound at a time, which is assessed, miked, processed, recorded, immediately reviewed, and repeated until the sound is satisfactory. This process affords the opportunity to strip away all distractions except getting a great sound in a simple focused recording scenario—and this will increase your proficiency.

Creative Miking

A lot of excellent samples have been captured utilizing one microphone and a good preamp. Everything we've covered in the *S.M.A.R.T. Guide* series is very important in the sampling process. Because during sampling you typically focus on one instrument, technique becomes even more important to the creation of interesting and sonically excellent samples.

Single Microphone Samples

In tracking a group, microphone distance choices are often based as much on isolation as they are on sound quality. In recording samples of individual instruments, the only thing that really matters is the audio quality of each sample. A tom, for example, requires a close miking technique in most live recording situations. However, in a sampling environment, you soon discover that the mic position that often sounds best is further from the drum.

Using one microphone, there is a broad range of sounds that can be captured from each sound source. The operating principle and miking distance combine to provide a specific sound. With each microphone, adjust the placement until you hear the sound you need. Aspects of the sample such as room ambience and intimacy are best captured in the sampling process, as long as they are integral to the emotion and urgency of the sound. If there is a question about how you envision the sound of the sample in your production, include minimal ambience, especially if a high-quality reverberation device could model a range of acoustic sounds that might be appropriate. The more practice you get, the better you'll get at guessing which mics and miking distances will sound good for each application.

Video Example 3-1

Comparison of Mic Distances from the Tom

Single Microphone Distance during Sampling

Miking a drumset in a close-mic application is different than sampling individual drums. While close-miking, separation between mics is important. The 3:1 rule tells us that the distance between any two mics should be at least three times the distance for each mic from its intended source. On the other hand, when sampling individual drums, all decisions about mic technique and choice are driven by sound quality.

When close-miking a tom, the mic is typically about two inches from the head. The photos below show the close mic along with two mic positions that typically sound better. The sound of most toms is best with a condenser mic placed between one and two feet from the drum. In addition, a moving-coil mic is typically best for close-miked applications. As the mic moves farther from the head, a large diaphragm condensor mic captures clean transients while providing a full, clean sound.

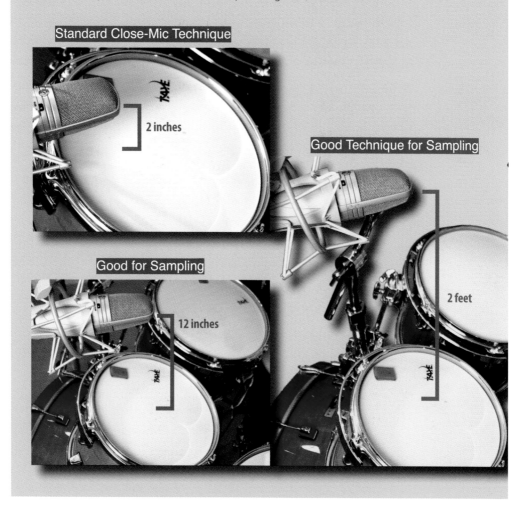

Standard Close-Mic Technique

2 inches

Good Technique for Sampling

2 feet

Good for Sampling

12 inches

Even though a single microphone is capable of providing excellent sampling results, multiple-mic setups hold far greater potential for capturing the depth and complexity of the audio source. If multiple microphones are summed to a mono channel, you have the opportunity to create a more interesting-sounding sample than with a single mic. If you record multitrack samples, where the mics are assigned to stereo or surround tracks, your samples will add amazing dimension and interest to your recordings.

Stereo Miking

The human hearing system is truly amazing. With two ears and a brain we are able to perceive right and left, as well as perceived room size, closeness, front, back, and immediate surrounding surface distances. It is and always has been the ideal to create a recorded listening experience that matches and exceeds an acoustic performance, but that's not as easy as one might think.

Simply placing two microphones in the same acoustic space doesn't guarantee a quality recording. You must consider the distance from each mic to the source, as well as the distance between the two microphones. You must also consider and assess the interactions of the sonic reflections off the immediate surrounding surfaces in the locations of the source and the two microphones.

The stereo miking techniques, which were covered in *The S.M.A.R.T. Guide to Mixers, Signal Processors, Microphones, and More*, as well as the techniques covered in *The S.M.A.R.T. Guide to Recording Great Tracks in a Small Studio*, are each crucial in the stereo sampling procedure.

If you're sampling an acoustic instrument in an acoustic space, listen to the instrument sound in the room. It's always a great idea to test a few different room locations. You'll be amazed at how the sound can change before you even place the microphones.

Stereo Miking Techniques for Sampling

Traditional stereo miking techniques work very well during a sampling session. The cymbals below will have a very natural left-right balance when miked with a standard X - Y configuration.

Non-traditional stereo techniques are also very appropriate during sampling. If you enjoy the ambient sound of your recording environment, try using one microphone for the direct intimate sound combined with a room mic. In practical use, the close mic is typically panned for proper placement and then the room mic is added in the same pan position until the desired blend is achieved.

Specifically when sampling cymbals, it is often effective to place one mic above the cymbal pointing down and one mic below pointing up. The sounds from the two mics are different, and one or the other might be perfect for your recording situation. Depending on the sound you want, you might need to invert the phase on the bottom mic when combining them to one track.

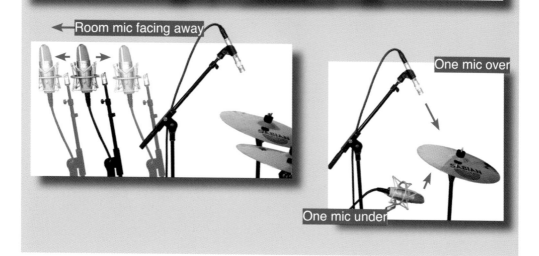

X - Y configuration

Room mic facing away

One mic over

One mic under

It isn't always necessary to use a standard stereo miking technique. Sometimes it's a great idea when recording stereo samples to set one microphone close to the source, to capture the intimacy of the sound, and one mic farther away from the source to capture the ambient sound. In using these samples, blend the close and distant mics to get the sound you need for the production. It is also very effective to pan the close and distant mics apart to increase the size and depth of the sound.

Listen to any instrument, sound effect, or voice with a few critical questions in mind.

+ What is the transient content? This question is an important indicator of the type of microphone that should produce the most accurate replication of the original sound. Sometimes you don't really want or need accuracy, so you might intentionally choose the wrong textbook choice just to see what the resulting sound is.

+ Is the sound edgy or smooth? Choose the microphone accordingly. Most ribbon mics and many large diaphragm condenser mics help smooth out an otherwise abrasive sound. Many moving-coil and small diaphragm condenser mics either accentuate an edgy sound or at least accurately capture it. If you've been progressing through this series, you've seen and heard proof that microphone selection is anything but a random decision. Mic characteristics can be predicted based on their operating principles. Use these characteristics to help build the perfect sound for your specific audio application.

Surround Miking

With the increased popularity of surround systems, it is becoming more likely that you'll need to know how to set up and record surround audio, whether for music, sound effects, or samples. The following

Surround Miking Techniques for Sampling

There are a couple very common surround techniques. The first is the coincident setup, which uses two X - Y configurations—one pointing forward and one pointing backward. Typically referred to as LRFB (left, right, front, back), this setup downmixes very well because of its excellent phase coherence. This configuration adapts accurately to mono, stereo, quad, 5.1, and 7.1.

Side View of LRFB

LRFB Mic Configuration

The VSA Tree

Another common setup spaces the left, center, and right microphones along the same arc with each mic about a foot apart—the left and right mics are angled apart by about 45 degrees and the center mic is aimed straight forward. The rear microphones are on the same plane but about two feet behind the front mics, pointing backwards. Typically the low-frequency component is taken from a low-pass filter of the other channels. The device shown (left) is the VSA Tree surround mic holder. This rack attaches to a mic stand with the mics aiming out across a horizontal plane.

standard surround-miking configurations have proven to provide an accurate and dependable sonic image. They translate well to surround playback systems, they tend to downmix well to stereo or mono, and they typically sound good.

Start with these techniques, and then add your own creative touch. Surround audio is common in film, television, and music. Many of these standard techniques provide accurate imaging in an acoustic environment—they typically feel like sonic reality. That is often the approach that works best for many applications, but sampling in surround provides the opportunity to experiment with unconventional techniques.

Ambience Microphones

Whether you're recording in mono, stereo, or surround, microphones set up to include natural room ambience can help add interest and individuality to your samples. If you're recording in a room that has a pleasing and interesting ambient quality, set up the close mics, and then set up a stereo pair of room mics distant from the sound source. Either blend the room mics in with the close mics, or in the case of surround samples, send the distant mics to the back or side speakers.

It is very common to set up ambient microphones when recording drums, guitars, and orchestral instruments. Often they add to the sonic impact, but sometimes they detract from the intimacy and overall power of the recording. Additionally, most symphonic, orchestral, and choral recordings are defined by the sound of the performance hall. On the other hand, in the popular music realm lead vocals, backing vocals, and most keyboard sounds are recorded in a way that minimizes all acoustic ambience. Any inclusion of natural ambience is carefully selected and then blended through the use of electronic simulation.

Including Reverberation and Delay Effects

Effects are an important part of a good sample performance patch in the same way that effects are important in any recording. Reverberation, delay effects, and dynamic effects all play important parts in defining each sample. However, as I previously mentioned, be sure to record and store the sample dry (without effects), either creating a new and separate patch that includes effects or leaving the choice and application of just the right effect until mixdown.

Including Dynamics Processors

In many sampling applications it's best to sample dry and flat. When no effects or equalization are applied during sampling, there is more freedom for sonic shaping during mixdown or tracking. High-definition samples provide ample signal-to-noise ratio to allow for natural raw samples recorded simply with a good mic and preamp. On the other hand, lower-resolution samples benefit greatly from the use of dynamics control during recording. Much like the process of recording as hot as possible to analog tape (without overloading) in order to keep the signal as far as possible from the noise floor, using dynamic control during sampling helps keep the low-level portions of the sample from being confused and masked by the minimum-bit portions of the digital words. As the compressor/limiter controls the loudest portions of the audio being sampled, the softest parts are turned up when the controlled level is made up to restore the peaks to full digital level.

No matter what the sampling resolution, there is one very positive result realized when you include dynamics control in your sampling procedure: The sampled sounds are more polished, refined, and profes-sional-sounding. It is quite a benefit when the samples are ready to go right out of the chute.

From a purist's standpoint, the sample should be as natural as possible, leaving sound changes and effects for later in the recording process. From a realist's standpoint, the more polished the sampled sound is, the more likely that it will sound great in context, thus there will be an increased likelihood that it will be put to use in an efficient and creative manner.

Dynamics Control during Sampling

The number of bits in a digital audio word represents its dynamic resolution—the number of discrete steps from full digital level to silence. A 24-bit word provides a resolution of 16,777,216 steps, whereas an 8-bit word provides a resolution of 256 steps.

If you're recording a sample that has a wide dynamic range with a substantial amount of audio detail at very low amplitude, consider using a compressor or limiter during the sampling process. The least sonically accurate digital recordings are of low-amplitude sounds because they typically reside in the lower eight bits of the dynamic resolution. Listen to any audio recorded at eight bits or less to immediately understand the corresponding decrease in audio quality, when compared to 16- or 24-bit recordings.

A compressor/limiter reduces the dynamic range so there is less difference between the softest and loudest sound. This enables you to boost the signal into the sampler so the softer sounds are relatively increased in amplitude. With proper use, dynamics control could help move your minimum-amplitude audio from the bottom six bits well up toward nine, 12, or even 16 bits.

The highlighted area in the illustration (right) compares the amplitude of the quiet parts of this audio segment before and after compression. After compression the entire recording level can be increased for optimum level. Therefore, the level of the quiet portions dramatically increases so they are represented by an increased number of digital bits. This results in greater sonic detail throughout the sample.

The pictured sample demonstrates nearly a 400-percent level increase during the highlighted region.

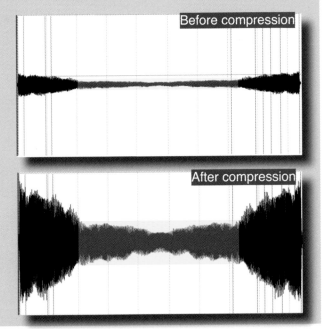

Before compression

After compression

Equalization during Sampling

Equalization is frequently applied to the sound source while it's being sampled. For the simple fact that a refined and polished sound is easier to use, moderate equalization is often applied during sampling. Pragmatically speaking, an appropriately equalized sound is easier to incorporate into any production. For those who want ultimate control, even at the expense of ease of use, equalization decisions are typically reserved for critical decisions during mixdown or tracking.

It is possible to operate optimally with your list of samples. Record the raw sample data, and then save the sample in several different forms. Include multiple versions of the raw sample—use dynamic processing, reverberation effects, delay effects, and equalization, saving each variation under the same name and basic number, adjusting the sample name to indicate the variation included.

Get Some Completely Different Sounds

As you build a sample library, keep in mind that many awesome sounds consist of ingredients that provide emotion or imagery, yet they are barely audible in the overall sound. Film and television sound designers frequently used layered sounds designed to draw the viewer into the emotion of a scene. A scream or a lion's roar layered under an orchestral punch provides a completely different impression than the orchestral punch alone. The sound of a freight train combined with a very active percussive composition completely changes the listening and viewing experience.

Use your imagination. Whether you're working with sound design or music, build a library of sound effects that contain and express primal, instinctive emotion.

Here's a list of suggested sounds to add to your library. Start here, but ponder the depths of your own soul to find sounds that you associate with each emotion—fear, anger, love, desire, passion, sadness, or whatever comes to mind.

+ Any animal sounds
+ Any travel sounds (planes, trains, automobiles, and so on)
+ Opening things, such as doors, packages, cans of food, and so on
+ Dropping and breaking various materials
+ Hitting various items (experiment with items of several sizes and weights)
+ Body noises
+ Screams
+ Various tools (grinders, hammers, saws, ratchets, and so on)
+ Ambience from several commercial, professional, and private locations
+ Crowd noises

Most sound effects are commercially available and are typically found in packages. Many of these effects are very good; they represent natural and contrived sounds and support visual imagery very well.

Whenever you use a commercial effects library, be careful of two considerations in particular.

+ Read the legal material that accompanies the library. Many libraries that are available through regular commercial outlets, such as record stores, are not licensed for use in music production or projects that will be resold. These libraries are only meant for home use and entertainment. If you are using sound effects in commercially saleable projects, you must purchase a library that is licensed and released for such use. Many online companies offer royalty-free sound effects and music for sale that is immediately downloadable. An Internet search for "sound effects libraries" will provide ample resources for properly licensed, commercially produced effects.

* Once you begin your quest for the perfect sounds, you'll soon realize the daunting task of scouring through hundreds or even thousands of sounds. It can take hours to find a sound that is only barely acceptable. I find that it is often quicker and almost always more powerful to imagine the perfect sound and then simply record it. A laptop computer, a couple good mics, and a small portable interface, such as the Digidesign Mbox, are the perfect setup for recording high-quality sounds at home or in the field.

Video Example 3-2

Field Recording with PowerBook and Mbox

Sampler Parameters

Whether you're using a hardware- or software-based sampler, the same functions and controls play a key role in your efficiency. Once you learn the basics of this process, you can easily perform sampling tasks on any sampler you encounter.

Level Adjustment

In virtually all cases, samplers utilize standard peak meters. In the case of software-based samplers, you might be given the option to choose between peak meters and average-level meters (such as the standard VU meter). If your meters are set to read average signal strength, you won't be accurately judging the peak level of the transients, which can easily exceed the average by nine or more decibels. In most cases, you'll get better results monitoring signal level through a peak meter because the main consideration in digital recording is to avoid clipping the input.

Recording Process

A few options and considerations are unique to the sampling process in some cases. However, there is no secret process that results in wonderful-sounding samples other than the utilization of great sound sources, stellar gear, brilliant technique, and inspired creativity.

Manual Recording

Recording audio into a sampler is identical in basic functionality to recording audio into any digital recorder. Simply provide a signal to the sampler input, set the record level, and press Record to start and Stop to end recording.

Assigning the Root Key

The root key is the single key that plays the sample at the exact pitch that it was originally recorded. One of the first tasks in sampling is selecting the note (the MIDI key) that plays the original sample.

Auto Record Start/Trigger

Virtually all samplers, since the very first Fairlight, provide an option to automatically trigger recording. In this process, the record threshold is set just above the ambient noise floor. Once the desired sound surpasses the threshold level, recording begins. This is a convenient feature because it automatically trims excess sound off the front of the sample, which results in two positive benefits.

+   Disk space and RAM are not wasted as the sampler records room ambience waiting for the desired sound. This was even more

Dynamic Triggering during Sampling

A traditional sampler parameter is the trigger level, which is simply an audio gate that restricts recording until the audio signal exceeds the user-set threshold. This feature helps eliminate dead space before the sample and, when set properly, results in a sample that begins playback as soon as you press the corresponding key on the MIDI keyboard.

Notice the sound wave below. The first few seconds are room ambience alone, then the target sound begins about half way through the illustration. Setting the threshold of the sample trigger just above the ambience delays the sample start until the onset of the audio source.

important when RAM was small and expensive, and when disk space was harder to come by.

 ♦ Because the excess was not recorded, the sample begins playing as soon as the assigned key is pressed. Even a one-second space at the beginning of a sample is cumbersome when you're trying to review the sample.

The record trigger feature is most convenient when you are using a hardware sampler. If you're sampling a snare drum, for instance, you can get the levels set and then press the Record button. As you get in place the sampler waits patiently, then starts recording as you strike the drumhead.

The primary negative aspect of the auto-record process is the loss of important data in the onset of the source sound. If the threshold is not set perfectly, the sample, although otherwise wonderful, might be useless. Always guess low on the threshold setting. Adjust it lower and lower until the ambient room sounds trigger the start of recording, and then raise it a bit. This will usually suffice, although you may experience a few false starts.

Editing the Sample

Once the sample is recorded, it needs to be trimmed and prepared for efficient and convenient playback. There are many parameters available on the modern sampler to help shape the sound. Most of them are common to the recording process in general, but some are specific to sample manipulation.

Sample Start and End Times

Even though samplers provide the record trigger, there are some sounds that fade in, rendering the trigger useless. Also, at the end of each sample the signal is recorded until you physically stop recording. Furthermore, when using a software sampler you typically have more to work with in terms of storage, RAM, and processing power, so the auto trigger is almost irrelevant.

Once you have completed the sample recording, most systems provide a graphic of the waveform to assist in the editing process. This aids in the process of trimming the excess off the start and end of the sample. Many of the original samplers did not provide graphic capabilities, so the waveform editing process was inaccurate, time consuming, and often very frustrating.

Simply select the starting and ending points for your sampled sound. They are indicated by a large number, which references the positions according to the actual sample number along the horizontal timeline. The best places to start and end samples are at the point where the waveform crosses the zero amplitude line. This is fairly easy to see on the graphic display; however, most modern samplers provide a selection that automatically forces the start and end times to the closest zero location. This selection is, oddly enough, usually labeled "Zero."

Truncate

Once the start and end points are chosen, the sample can be performed as is with no further alteration, or you can choose to truncate the sound. Truncation erases all data before the start point and after the end point. Typically, there is an option to completely discard the unwanted audio, or—this is the more intelligent choice—the truncation can simply create a new sample that consists of the data between the start and end points. In this way, the new sample is placed on a new section of the keyboard for performance, while the original complete sample is still available for performance at its original location. This is a fundamental aspect of the sampling process.

Truncating the Sample

Truncating, an editing procedure that is performed once the sample has been recorded, simply involves removing the unwanted audio before and after the sampled sound. For two reasons in particular, each sample should be truncated.

1. Removing non-crucial audio from all samples decreases the amount of data, so each sample occupies a smaller amount of the storage medium.

2. Truncating results in efficient and musical playback. Truncate the dead space from the start of the sample so that as soon as the MIDI key is pressed, the sample begins playback. Truncate the end of the sample to eliminate any unwanted noise or extraneous sounds during playback.

The highlighted areas of the original sample waveform (below) indicate extraneous audio, unnecessary to musical implementation.

Notice the truncated sample contains only the desired portion of the sample. Truncation is typically a permanent and destructive action—the audio you trim from the beginning and end of the original sample cannot be restored. It's always a good idea to save the original sample audio, in case you want to adjust the truncation at a later date.

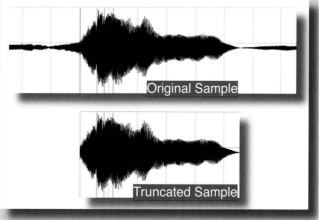

Options are provided in the truncation process that specify where data before the start point, after the end point, or both before the start point and after the end point is eliminated. It is generally best to define the range of the waveform you want to keep and truncate everything else.

Normalize

Samplers have most of the same controls found on any hardware- or software-based digital recorder. The normalize control evaluates the sound wave's peak amplitude, then boosts the entire waveform level so that peak level is at full digital level.

Normalizing the waveform provides a means to set every sample so its level is full and strong. However, normalizing a waveform that was recorded at artificially low levels really only boosts the level of a low-resolution digital recording—it will still tend to sound grainy, noisy, or distant. Your samples will sound much better if you actually record them at a full digital level than if you merely achieve a strong level by normalizing.

Often, samples that are used together across the MIDI keyboard vary in level because the specific ingredients of the sampled instrument acoustically blend together in a very natural way—even though their technical levels are inconsistent. When setting up multisamples across the keyboard, the volume of each sample can be adjusted, so you could recreate the original balance to simulate an authentic sound; however, within a reasonable dynamic range, you'll achieve more believable results if you maintain the authentic dynamic relationship during sampling. Especially if you're using high-resolution audio, resist the temptation to normalize every sample simply to maximize the level.

Multisampling Layout

You'll soon find that most natural sounds only sound good on a few keys when played from a MIDI keyboard. For the sounds you sample in normal operation, the sample will raise and lower in pitch a half step at a time as you play up and down the keyboard. Depending on the type of sampled sound, there is typically little use in playing the sample over the range of more than an octave. Because this is the case, multisampling is provided to let you spread several samples across the MIDI keyboard. In theory, you could assign a sample to each key on the keyboard.

Because certain sounds don't sound right when raised and lowered in pitch, samplers provide an option to spread the sample out over several keys, yet force the playback to always output the original sample, unaltered by pitch change. This option is usually called *constant pitch*.

Multisample mode is critical to getting the most authentic-sounding sample of instruments with a complex waveform, or instruments such as drums and percussion that have many different sounds in a kit form. Sampling a guitar or piano requires several samples across the range of the instrument or each performance variance.

A piano sounds different when it is struck with power and force than it does when played lightly with great sensitivity. To build an excellent piano sample, record a new sample for each two or three notes playing forcefully, and then record a new set of samples striking the keys with medium force. Finally, record yet another set of samples striking the keys very lightly. This is the minimum requirement for a believable sampled piano. You really should record another set of identical samples with the soft pedal depressed and the lid raised and lowered. In addition, the more individual samples you can record across the instrument range, the better. The sampling process is often very tedious, especially when it is done well.

Mutisampling across the MIDI Keyboard

In many situations, several samples should be spaced out across the keyboard. When sampling drums, for instance, place all of the ingredients in separate ranges. Enable each drum for playback from multiple keys. In this way, each sample offers pitch options for meeting the sonic needs of more recording situations. The illustration below demonstrates a multisample that has been intentionally distributed across the MIDI keyboard.

The Mach 5 screen below demonstrates a drumset multisample with each drum spread across two or more keys. A setup like this results in maximum flexibility and easy of use. The included instruments are

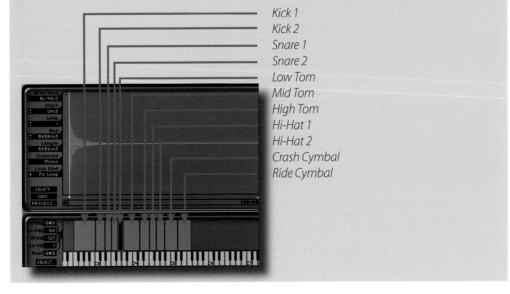

Kick 1
Kick 2
Snare 1
Snare 2
Low Tom
Mid Tom
High Tom
Hi-Hat 1
Hi-Hat 2
Crash Cymbal
Ride Cymbal

There are usually controls provided for varying the pitch and volume level of each sample across the multisample keyboard. Whether you're sampling grand piano or banjo, you need to be prepared to perform several samples to accurately imitate any wide-range instrument.

Storing

Once the sample is completed and finely polished, be sure it is saved using a standard numbering and labeling procedure such as the one referenced in this chapter. It's a great idea to store the sample as soon as it has been recorded. As you shape the sample and add multiple samples across the keyboard, either overwrite (replace) the original sample or save the updated version under a different name (possibly the same name with a successive numerical indication).

Keep the raw data in its original form if at all possible. Once it has been recorded, you might be amazed at the myriad possibilities for interesting sounds that are provided in the audio outside your initial usable range.

Looping

In relation to sampling, looping simply replays a specified portion of the sampled waveform over and over as long as the key is held down. A loop is created that circulates over and over. There is also capacity provided to instruct the playback to loop back and forth between the specified beginning and end of the loop. The audio actually plays forward, then backward, then forward, then backward, and so on.

Creating a Long Tone

There are a few applications for the looping process, one of which is creating a long sustained tone from a short sample. Historically, this technique has been used to help minimize the sample length and therefore the burden on the processor, RAM, and storage device.

To create a usable loop that sounds as if you're just holding out a natural sound, you must carefully choose the loop point. Looping between the beginning and end of one completion of a waveform should, in theory, provide the sound of the waveform as long as the pitch is constant. In reality, looping only one instance of the sound-wave cycle produces a very motionless, lifeless, and static sound. This sound can often be given life through the incorporation of an oscillator (such as the LFO) that varies the pitch or volume continuously and slightly. However, better results can often be realized when larger sections of the sample are looped. Loop points are set in the same way as the sample start and end times; they must be carefully selected to ensure a smooth, glitch-free, and believable long tone.

Video Example 3-3

Creating a Long Tone

Looping a Groove

Possibly the most common usage of the term "loop" refers to digitally recorded drum grooves that are used to supply the rhythmic foundation for many home and professional recording projects. This is simply the same process used to define a waveform to loop for creation of a long tone from a short recording. In this case you simply define a larger piece of audio, usually two or four measures long. The loop plays over and over, creating a constant rhythmic background.

Drum loops have become very popular because they're easy to use and because they sound far better than a drum sound in a typical drum machine, keyboard, or sound module. A true loop playback program provides for seamless tempo changes and high-quality, real drum sounds. Apple's GarageBand software is a very easy-to-use example of loop playback software. It contains many audio and MIDI loops that sound great, and they all follow the song tempo.

Loops are not limited to drums. It's also common to see two-, four-, or eight-bar riffs, comps, and strum patterns from virtually any instrument. Using several of these loops, you can construct very authentic-sounding and believable recordings without ever playing a note on a real instrument.

Crossfades

One of the concerns in looping waveforms or longer musical segments is the elimination of awkward clicks, pops, or textural changes as playback crosses from the end point of the loop back to the start point of the loop. In an effort to eliminate these unwanted sounds, crossfades are provided, which fade the end of the loop out across the fade in of the beginning of the loop.

Whether you're looping a tone, a groove, or a small riff, the crossfade option can help smooth out the loop point so it is sonically invisible. Keep in mind, though, that this continual crossfade process uses up computational power. If your sampler or computer is running on the verge of being overtaxed, your time might be well spent by adjusting the loop point so crossfades are unnecessary.

Sampling Grooves

There are many commercial sample libraries you can purchase specifically as loops to incorporate into your sampler system. Many samplers automatically accept virtually any sample format. The samples are incorporated in an architecture that compensates for the sequence tempo, following along with other tracks in perfect time. Time compression and expansion occurs to compensate for tempo changes, while the original recording's pitch and timbre are unaltered.

Keep in mind that any time you stretch or compress the timeline of any digital audio recording beyond reason, sound quality suffers. Even though the sound seems to hold up to extreme changes, certain ingredients are degrading. If you are recording a high-resolution production, use high-resolution loops and avoid extreme alterations. Eventually you'll realize a decrease in sonic transparency and purity, as well as the precision of positioning in the stereo or surround panorama.

Prerecorded Sample Libraries

Some libraries are nothing more than high-quality stereo or surround recordings of individual instruments, voices, or sound effects recorded and isolated specifically for the purpose of sampling. Whereas many libraries are tagged with tempo data and other information that facilitates automatic changes in relation to the sequence tempo, these libraries only provide sounds that you can record into your hardware or software sampler.

These libraries have great value, especially for those with minimal recording equipment. Access to professionally recorded instrument sounds is not only convenient, but also provides an efficient means of creating great-sounding loops.

Most of the grooves and sample material will be marked with tempo specifications. If the sample was recorded at 110 bpm, set the tempo of your sampler to 110 bpm. This way, most digital recording software or sampling devices can at the very least manually adjust the loop tempo to fit the sequence tempo.

A wonderful benefit of these libraries is that they typically offer several variations of each loop, either separately or as a result of a continuous live performance of a single musical idea. As the riff is performed over and over, subtle nuances are included that offer the live feel, which provides power and emotion to any song. In addition, these libraries are typically royalty-free. Once you purchase the library, you can use it guilt-free on any project you want, whether commercial or personal.

Companies like Big Fish Audio, Native Instruments, and Spectrasonics set the pace for high-quality sample and loop libraries. Each of these companies provide an excellent (and very user-friendly) virtual sampler that enables your DAW to perform as an extremely powerful sampler. Their libraries are truly amazing, featuring world-class sounds as performed by world-class musicians. These powerful tools, combined with excellent musical taste and traditionally tested production concepts and techniques, provide ample resources for music development and production.

Samples and loops are available in multiple formats to fit almost any digital system need, although most systems function perfectly well with Audio Units, WAV, Acid, and Rex formats.

Sample categories cover a wide range of musical applications, from drums and percussion to brass, strings, woodwinds, and vocals. Additionally, most styles are addressed, such as hip-hop, rock, big band, pop, jazz, blues, and so on.

Video Example 3-4

Sample Libraries from Big Fish Audio, Native Instruments, and Spectrasonics

Sampling from Commercially Released CDs and Records

In the early years of accessible samplers, no one thought much about finding a great isolated drum groove in a great-sounding record and sampling it for use in a recording, whether commercial or personal. That soon changed because the legal system quickly reinforced the notion that stealing a little bit of a song is just as bad as stealing the whole song.

It is wrong to simply sample bits of a commercially released recording. However, if you really want to use something from a recording, contact the artists or their legal representation and ask for permission. If you have a recording of a local or regional group or soloist, you might be able to use parts of the recording for little or no money. If you want to sample part of a major release, you should expect to pay handily. Also, expect to hear from the original artist's lawyers if your song becomes a hit, even if you got previous clearance.

If you obtain permission to sample from a finished CD, you'll probably find many amazing sounds that can be sampled and manipulated. Once you become proficient at the sampling procedure, you'll begin to understand that often the best sounds are created from unlikely sources. When manipulated in a fresh and creative way, a vocal breath, guitar string squeak, or even simply a portion of a riff could become an amazing sound. Often these unexpected sound creations contain a hidden power and emotion provided by the root of the sample.

Sampling Your Recordings of Grooves

Once you've completed several recordings, you'll probably have your own arsenal of excellent riffs and grooves. As long as you own them, separate them out of your mixes and build your own library. If it's a good enough library, you might eventually be able to sell it. Good, fresh-sounding loops are often hard to find.

Most of the time it's most convenient to prepare stereo mixes of the instruments to be recorded or imported into your sampler. Although mono sounds are typically made to feel stereo through tasteful application of effects, a good stereo sample provides an impact that surpasses most mono recordings.

If you are using sampling software that is capable of playing surround samples, set up some surround recordings as describe previously and capture the ambient life of a great room or hall along with your instrumental or vocal performances.

Some libraries are available in multitrack format, specifically for high-powered samplers or digital recording software packages. In the case of drums, you receive eight tracks that include separate tracks for each drum along with overheads or room mics. Often these drum parts are played in eight-bar phrases with textural changes made to indicate common musical sections, such as verse, chorus, bridge, solo, intro, and outro.

Often the line blurs between powerful samplers and digital recording software. They're really essentially the same tools with mostly the exact same capabilities. The primary differences are that a sampler is, by definition, triggered to play samples from a MIDI keyboard, and a sampler playback originates in RAM whereas a DAW playback ultimately comes from the hard drive.

Custom Samples

There are so many available sound libraries that you might think you would never need to create a sample yourself. In reality, once you envision the perfect sound for your music, you could spend hours looking for just the right sound, only to come up empty-handed. Once you can hear the sound you want in your head, set up your mics and record it for yourself, either directly into your sampler or into your digital recording software. Custom samples are typically the most appropriate for your music. In addition, the sampling process forces you to focus on getting the very best sound possible from whatever sound source you're using.

Working from the Audio Inputs

Modern samplers provide both mic and line inputs. There is often a switch to select the input status, so the same actual input is used for both mic- and line-level signals. Be sure to select the appropriate status. As you've already seen in *The S.M.A.R.T. Guide to Mixers, Microphones, Signal Processors, and More*, microphone output signals are approximately 30 to 60 dB colder than standard line-level signals. A microphone plugged into a line-level input won't have enough signal to obtain a sufficient level—a line- level signal plugged into a microphone input will overdrive the input, even at the most modest levels.

Mic Inputs

A very important consideration when plugging a mic into a sampler audio input is the microphone operating principle. Condenser microphones require phantom power, yet some sampler mic inputs

Audio Inputs on the Hardware Sampler

Audio inputs on most hardware samplers are compatible with mic-level or line-level signals. Typically, a switch selects the input type for your application. Be sure you have chosen properly. An instrument connected to a mic-level input provides a signal that is too strong—it will overdrive the input. If a microphone is plugged into a line-level input the signal is insufficient.

Many samplers do not provide phantom power. Therefore, if you're sampling with a condensor mic you'll probably need to use battery power or an external phantom power supply.

Mic/Line Switch

- When sampling instruments and outputs from mixers and outboard equipment select "Line."
- When sampling any signal from a microphone select "Mic."

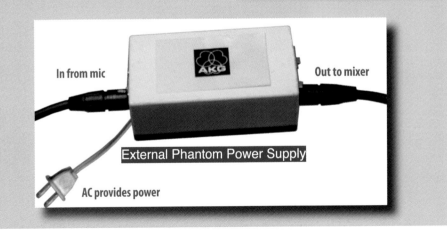

In from mic
Out to mixer
External Phantom Power Supply
AC provides power

don't supply phantom power. Without power the condenser mic will not work. Unfortunately, many samples are perfectly suited for recording through a condenser mic.

To use a condenser mic with a non-powered input, there are three options.

+ Use batteries.

+ Use an external phantom power supply. These devices plug into AC power to access power for the mic. The mic cable plugs from the mic to the phantom power supply, and another cable patches into the sampler input.

+ Use a mixer that supplies phantom power. Plug the mic into the mixer and then patch from the mixer into the sampler input. Many mixers provide a switch to set the main output of a small mixer to either mic- or line-level. Be sure that the mixer output matches the sampler input.

Line Inputs

Much creative flexibility and sonic-shaping potential is gained through the use of a high-quality mixer patched into the sampler line input. A good mixer probably contains a higher-quality mic preamp than the sampler; the mixer equalization helps shape the sounds, and the mixer is a very convenient monitoring source once the sample process is completed.

For very easy and convenient sampling, patch the outputs from a couple mixer aux buses into the hardware sampler inputs. This way, any time you want to sample any sound that's running through your mixer, simply turn the track or tracks up in the specified aux bus or buses to send the signal to the sampler inputs, adjust the levels, and then record the sample. This scenario offers the potential for some nasty feedback loops. Because of this, be certain that the aux buses are muted on the sampler input channels.

Another very effective technique that results in some of the most amazing samples involves the use of a high-quality external mic preamp patched directly into the sampler line input. For those with access to excellent microphones and preamplifiers (whether vintage or new), compare various combinations. Listen carefully and find the best sound possible—it will make a big difference in the sound of your music.

Connect Auxiliary Outputs to the Sampler Line Input

Consider patching the output of a stereo aux bus to the sampler's line input. This is a very convenient setup. The fact that the mixer is always connected to the sampler audio input is very efficient. Anytime you want to sample audio coming into mixer, simply turn up the appropriate auxiliary sends until the optimum level is sent to the sampler audio inputs.

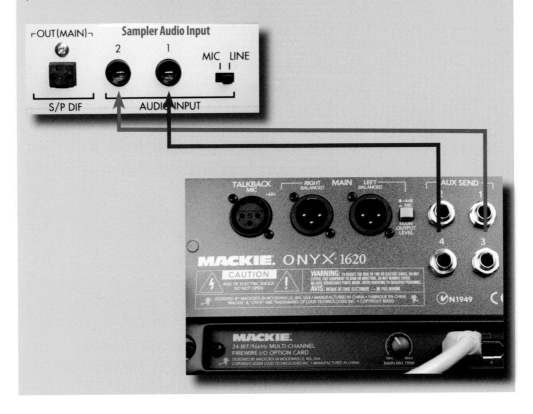

There is a fundamental problem with using the sampler's microphone input or a live mic through a mixer patched into the line inputs: inconsistent performance. Recording a live source, although it is often fresh and electrifying, is less efficient than recording from a prerecorded source. In most cases, it's a good idea to record a few minutes of the source, whether to analog or digital media, and then choose the perfect segments to sample. Once the appropriate performances are located, patch the playback device into the line input for audio sampling or export the segments for importing into the sampler. If your sampler displays the audio waveform graphically, it is possible to record long segments into the sampler to be cut into separate sample segments internally. If your sampler has sufficient RAM and processing power this is a viable option; however, in most hardware-based samplers, it's a good idea to avoid recording unnecessary audio. Prudent use of memory and media space is important to the power user.

Using Digital Recording Software with a Sampler

By far, the most powerful sampling process uses digital recording software. Everything you already know about your recording software applies to recording and editing samples. Whether you're using a hardware- or software-based sampler, take advantage of the power and convenience of your digital recording software.

Hardware-Based Sampling

Because modern hardware samplers accommodate most digital audio formats, use your digital recording software to record the sounds. RAM and hard disk space are in abundance in most software-based recorders, so you can afford to be a bit more liberal in your recording practice. Record multiple takes of your source. For example, if you're sampling a snare drum record several hits, including loud, medium, and soft hits along with rim shots, cross-rim sticking, buzz rolls, open rolls, and press rolls. Once you're satisfied with the sounds, trim and export each hit to whatever audio format you want.

The beauty of this system is that it offers speed, excellent sonic quality, and efficiency. After the samples are perfected, organized, and exported, they can be stored on CD, DVD, hard disk, or floppy disks. Modern samplers typically provide for connection of many types of storage devices, so importing the finished samples should be simple and quick.

Software-Based Sampling

Sampling from within your digital recording software using a software-based sampler is the ultimate in sampling experiences. Typically, audio is first recorded, edited, and processed in the normal manner, and then individual samples are separated, trimmed, and organized. To import the individual samples, simply open the sampling plug-in and drag the samples into the sampler screen. Samples open immediately in a graphic window, where they can be further trimmed, looped, or processed. Multisamples are either automatically assigned to the MIDI keyboard or they can be manually placed. Changes in the sample ranges or keyboard layout are very easy to perform.

Software samplers typically provide multiple filters and effects processors, so shaping the sound is visual and efficient. Most modern synthesizers use samples as a basis for most of their sounds, even if they don't actually sample audio, so incorporating filters, oscillators, and effects is very similar to the process at which you might already be proficient.

Video Example 3-5

Demonstrations of Software-Based Sampling

Rhythm Section and Vocal Sampling

As the sampling phenomenon has increased over the years, sampling has become a huge part of the recording process. Whether your musical genre is country, pop, techno, or rock, many of the sounds you hear in your favorite music are likely to be sampled.

The Function of Samples in Production

Samples are used heavily in high-budget productions as well as low-budget home studio productions. Drum samples are very commonly used in the commercial pop and country genres. In fact, they're used less in programming than they are in replacing the sounds of the original drum recordings.

It's common to utilize a MIDI trigger that responds to audio signals to plot the exact point when each drum was hit. Once the MIDI note map is completed, drum samples are easily triggered directly from the sequencing software. Toms that originally sounded small and clunky soon become huge. A tom that is recorded within the context of a complete kit recording sometimes lacks the depth and impact of a tom that's recorded alone in a great room, using microphone and placement techniques that are perfect for the sound, rather than perfect for minimal leakage.

Drum sounds can be virtually perfected through the use of samples and drum replacement, but sometimes that's a good thing and sometimes it's bad. Some genres such as jazz, guitar-driven rock, and alternative music thrive on the naturalness of a real recording. In fact, processing of the original recording is sometimes frowned upon.

You must be familiar with the genre you're recording or producing. Your decisions must be based on accepted procedures, yet you must always remain open to the creative use of any technique.

The Importance of Building the Right Sound for a Song

Music is, in essence, performed emotion. A love song is nothing without love, a sad song is nothing without sadness, an angry song is nothing without anger, and so on. Happy sounds don't work very well in sad songs, and sad sounds don't work well in happy songs. Many new producers or engineers don't really think about this stuff intentionally, although almost everyone instinctively knows it. On the other hand, if you are consciously aware of the emotion in a song—and if you do your best to find sounds that precisely match the feeling in the song—you might be amazed at the impact your production has on listeners.

For the next song you record, try tapping into the song's emotional feeling. Design some sounds that are inspired by your understanding of the lyrics. It's usually a good idea to make a list of the feelings invoked by the lyrics along with the sounds that evolve out of those feelings, much as you did in Chapter 1. Again, at first write fast and don't dwell on deep thoughts. Get the list going. You will get past the obvious choices into the more inspired and deep impressions. As your list grows, review it and really ponder each sound you've come up with.

Typically, your initial thoughts will each inspire a brand new list. Spend some time on this, but don't get stuck thinking so hard that you can't act. If you like an idea, start trying to work out the sound.

Building sounds that truly fit the music you're recording is a worthwhile activity—the song will turn out better and you'll get practice at creating sounds based on feelings.

Sampling Drums and Percussion

Drum and percussion sounds are well suited to the sampling process. They're short, their sounds are interesting and unique, they typically play easily from a keyboard or trigger pad, and several sounds can be laid out across the keyboard, providing multiple versions of each sound.

Mic Choice

Condenser microphones are always an excellent choice for sampling drums because almost all drums and percussion instruments contain strong, clean transients. Whereas in a complete recording of a drum kit moving-coil mics are often used in close proximity on the kick, snare, and toms, sampling affords the opportunity to mic from greater distances of a foot or two while using large- or small-capsule condenser mics to capture a full, warm sound with an excellent transient.

Because you're spending some time focusing on each sound, always strive for the best sound possible. In addition, be creative with your choices—try some different setups to see whether you can come up with an exciting new approach. Set up a stereo pair of mics in one of the standard configurations. Also, break out of the mold and try something different.

Sometimes it's a good idea to set one mic close to the source you're sampling, along with a stereo pair of mics farther back in the room. The stereo mics should be panned hard left and right, and the close mic should be panned center. Depending on the method of sampling you're using, blend the mics for the perfect sound going into the sampler audio inputs, record them to separate tracks on your digital recording software, or record all three mics to multiple tracks in your sampler.

Some modern hardware samplers provide four or more audio inputs. If you're using a powerful software-based sampler, capacity for surround samples up to 7.1 are common. Most professional-quality digital recording software will record and play back full 5.1 or 7.1 surround sound, including surround effects. This surround capability is another advantage of recording your sample material on a digital recording program and then preparing it for sampling.

Audio Example 4-1

Close Snare Mic with Stereo Room Mics

Record Levels

Because sampling is nothing more than digital recording, set levels so that the peak level doesn't overload the input. If you're sampling a live performance, you must leave headroom in the level you set, just in case the performer plays or sings louder than you expect. In any digital recording, the goal is to record the strongest level in the track at full digital level so you know you've optimized the full number of bits in the word.

Recording at artificially low levels results in a sound that is more

Adding a Stereo Pair of Room Mics to the Sample

To add a natural dimension to the sample, combine the single close microphone with a stereo pair of room mics. This techniques works well when sampling most instruments, although the results are typically most satisfying on drums and loud electric guitars. Some instruments, such as acoustic guitar and voice, are better-suited to the intimacy of close miking in most situations.

Pan the close mic to the center poition and then pan the two room mics hard left and right. Blend the room mics for the appropriate sound. If you're using a stereo sampler, make sure you're optimizing your sampling session by saving a sample of the blended stereo sound along with samples of the close mic and the stereo room mics alone—you might need a different blend on future projects.

Experiment with different placement and techniques for the room mics. An X-Y coincident pair works well and maintains phase coherence, but random placement often tends to widen the image. To increase the effective size of the room, use cardioid room mics and aim them away from the instrument, at a wall. Since the sound behind the mic is diminished due to off-axis discrimination, the direct sound from the instrument is minimized. The distance from the source is increased to the sum of the distance from the source to the wall and the distance from wall back to the microphone.

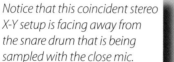

Notice that this coincident stereo X-Y setup is facing away from the snare drum that is being sampled with the close mic.

grainy-sounding and noisy than it should be. With this in mind, it's easy to see that sampling a sound you previously recorded to CD, DVD, or hard disk is more consistent and reliable than sampling a live performance. Simply replay the CD over and over until you have the perfect level set, and then record the sample.

Dynamic and Effects Processing

If you're recording live drums and percussion for sampling, it's a good idea to include compression or peak limiting in the signal path. This helps reduce the chances of overloading the input. Set the threshold so that the limiter only affects the peak levels. Any extreme compression or limiting should be reserved for application during mixdown. If you apply too much dynamic control during tracking it is very difficult to undo later, and an otherwise excellent recording could be rendered useless.

Layering Sounds and Multiple Velocity Triggering

Typically, a note that is played softly sounds different than a note that's played loudly and then turned down—the tonal color changes. For this reason, it's a good idea to sample the instrument at least at loud, medium, and soft performance levels. Most samplers allow samples to be layered, with different key velocities assigned to the various layers. With this setup, assign the strongest velocity to the strongest performance, the medium velocity to the medium performance, and the weakest velocity to the lightest note. The more divisions you make in the velocity scale (0–127), the more authentic and convincing your sample will be.

Audio Example 4-2

Layered Sounds with Multiple Velocities

Layering Samples with Multiple Velocities

The natural sound of a live musician performing music involves much more than notes and rhythms. The musical performance is made of heartfelt nuance, including constant changes in volume, timbre, and pitch as well as frequent musical inflections such as bends, scoops, glissandos, slides, and so on.

Samplers accomodate these musical ingredients through layered velocities. Assign several separate samples to the same root key, then adjust the velocity of each sample so that it will be played only in a specific velocity range. The root key is the single key that plays the sample at the exact pitch that it was originally recorded. If you've sampled a fretted guitar note six times (including a range of four volumes, a hammer on, and a trill), try assigning each version to its own discrete range of the 127 MIDI velocity values like the recommendations below.

- *Quietest note: Velocity range from 1 – 29*
- *Next loudest note: Velocity range from 30 – 50*
- *Next loudest note: Velocity range from 51 – 75*
- *Loudest note: Velocity range from 76 – 95*
- *Hammer on: Velocity range from 96 – 115*
- *Trill: Velocity range from 116 – 127*

The MIDI keyboards (below) represent samples at each horizontal and vertical division. Vertical segments indicate the note range for each sample root; horizontal segments represent velocity ranges. The easiest way to perform samples for this manner of sampling is to record all sample options together, playing each note several times—play through all volumes and nuances for each note and then extract each sample from the master recording, assigning each to the appropriate root key and velocity range.

Notice the bottom keyboard has one note selected, indicated by the purple highlighted box above F#4. This box indicates one of six velocity ranges, with the values of the selected box displayed along the left side of the keyboard. This selected box indicates that

- *The sample ranges from F#4 to G4.*
- *The root key is F#4.*
- *The note will only sound in response to velocities from 1 to 29.*

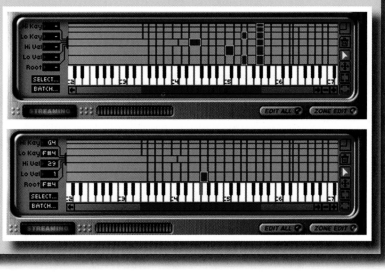

Sampling Drums

Drum and percussion sampling is common in daily sampler use. Because the drum sound defines the style, energy, and power of any production, high-quality, unique, and creative drum sounds are imperative.

Take your time. Focus on capturing drum sounds that are exciting to hear. Listen to your favorite recordings. There's a good chance that when you first heard them, something jumped out of the mix and caught your attention—something that was captivating. If you strive for sounds that impress your own musical senses and if you keep that as your standard throughout your productions, you'll eventually record music that competes in the musical marketplace.

When you are building a sample library, cover all your bases. You have the instruments miked and prepared, so capture multiple options, sample them, and save them under the same name with descriptive suffixes. Record a single hit, double hit, press, press roll, rim shot, cross-rim hit, and roll, as well as loud, medium, and soft hits.

Dynamics Processors and Drum Samples

Many commercial drum sounds are heavily compressed. Even though dynamics processors are often used during mixdown, there are several instances where compressing and limiting are appropriate during sampling.

Any time you're developing sounds for a live performance, do everything you can to record the sound that will work in that situation with no additional processing. Most modern hardware samplers provide processors onboard that are capable of reverberation and dynamics processing. On the other hand, most high-quality outboard processors sound better. Use your judgment and base your choice of action on the sound quality of the devices at hand.

As you develop the drum samples, record a sample with no processing at all and label it "dry" or "no_fx." Next, include a compressor/limiter in the signal path and build the sound that fills your need. If you have a few dynamics processors, compare them all to hear which one fits your application best. You might be surprised at the sonic difference. Given several hardware and software samplers, some will sound great while others will not be satisfactory.

Once you find the perfect sound, sample it. Then bracket your sample in the same way a photographer brackets each important shot. Because lighting is important to photographers, they typically take a picture at the proper aperture and shutter speed, and then they take a few shots with increased and decreased shutter and aperture settings. In the same way, after your sample is completed, build and sample sounds with slightly less and slightly more dynamics control. Because you've spent the time developing the sample, it's a simple task to sample more options for additional future uses.

Sampling Kick Drum

The kick drum sound is crucial in defining the low-frequency impact of a mix. There are several applications in which the kick sound must be huge and impressive and others in which it must be focused in a narrow bandwidth.

During sampling, your primary concern is developing the perfect sound, in contrast to tracking, when isolation is important. Mic placement is dependent on many of the same guidelines and considerations in either application. Aim the microphone at the center of the drum to capture the attack, or aim it at the outer edge of the head for more tone.

Several techniques that can help build an interesting and impressive sound are impossible, or at least impractical, when tracking an entire kit. Try some of the following techniques, and then develop some of your own.

Move the Mic away from the Kick

Move the mic away from the drum. Depending on whether the front head is on or off, you might find a sweet spot with the perfect blend of tone, attack, and ambience, or even miking from the beater side of the head.

Lengthen the Kick Drum

If you have an extra kick drum available, remove both heads and position it in front of the source kick. Place a mic at the end of the extra kick to get a deeper tone. If you don't have extra drums lying around, try building a tunnel out of various materials, such as cardboard, blankets, conduit, or any other material that effectively provides a tunnel, to help focus low-frequency energy. PVC duct material is available in 24-inch diameter. If you're serious about developing excellent kick drum samples, try miking at the end of two to four feet of this material, in front of the source kick.

Use Multiple Microphones

Position one mic close to the head inside the drum and one farther away. Blend them together for just the right combination of attack and room tone. Aim the inside mic at the center of the head where the beater hits for the most attack or toward the rim for more tone.

Experiment with distant position for the mic outside the kick. In most cases the outside mic interferes with the intimacy of the kick sound, so it might be blended lightly with the close mic just to provide a unique, interesting feeling.

If you're running out of tracks, you'll need to get the sound set up

Sampling the Kick Drum

When recording a kick drum, microphone choice and technique are critical. Each mic has a different characteristic sound and a distinct sonic variation caused by proximity and frequency content. The kick drum sound, like other drum sounds, contains more high-frequency and attack when miked at the center of the head; it also exhibits more low frequencies and tone when miked toward the shell.

Muffling systems, head choice, and drum size also play an important role in the recorded sound. It is difficult to get a great sound out of substandard kick drum; however, if you focus on proper tuning and sound control systems you should be able to find a sound that records easily and sounds very powerful, impressive, and distinct.

Aim mic toward the shell for more tone.

Aim mic toward the center for more attack.

To create a unique tone try extending the length of the kick drum by placing two drums together . This technique tends to deepen the drum tone.

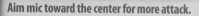

and combine both the inside and outside mics to one track. However, it's a better idea to print the outside mic to its own track so it can be blended in later if needed. If you feel you must commit and print both mics to a mono track, guess low on the room mic level. It's very difficult to compensate for a sound that contains too much ambience, but it's always easy to add reverb or natural ambience during mixdown.

Place Microphones in Common Containers

Each container provides a characteristic timbre. As a sound wave enters the container it reflects, summing and canceling at unique frequencies depending on the container size and material.

Position one mic close to the head and aim another mic into a coffee can, paint bucket, poster tube, or any other cylindrical or box-like item that might provide an interesting and unique tone.

This technique provides sonic content that is typically blended with the close mic to specifically add a unique flavor that is unattainable otherwise. In addition, given a full-range sound such as a complete drum set, acoustic guitar, and so on, the sound captured in these containers might provide an excellent breakdown sound, used to instantly change the texture and personality of your mix.

Audio Example 4-3

The Sound Variations from Different Mics on the Same Kick Drum

Video Example 4-1

Multiple Mics on the Kick Drum

Use Unconventional Microphones

The operating principle of the moving coil microphone is identical to the operating principle of the standard cone speaker. In both, a cylinder

Unconventional Mics on the Kick Drum

There are the accepted standard mics that adhere to conventional recording practice—they're predictable and usually produce a great sound. However, in a quest for a unique sound, try unconventional microphone choices and techniques.

The kick drum below is miked with an old mic I found in a vintage 1950s reel-to-reel tape recorder from Eicor. Since this is a sampling application I want to optimize the attack of the beater by placing the Eicor microphone on the beater side of the head, aimed at the point where the beater hits the head.

The kick drum to the right is being miked with a Yamaha NS-10 woofer. I wired this just like a microphone, with the output tabs on the speaker connected to pins two and three on the XLR connector and the cable shield connected to the speaker's metal frame.

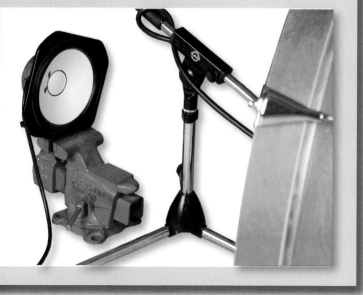

wound with copper wire moves around a magnet. One typically moves in response to audio stimulation (the microphone), and the other moves in response to changes in electrical energy (the speaker). However, a microphone will function as a tiny, quiet speaker, and a speaker will function as a rather slow and cumbersome microphone.

Try using a speaker as a microphone when you are looking for a big, beefy kick-drum sound. Combine it with a close mic aimed to capture the attack and presence, and you just might find the kick sound you've been looking for all your life.

The most common approach to this technique uses a woofer from one of the most popular studio monitors—the Yamaha NS-10. Simply connect the positive and negative speaker leads to pins two and three of a male XLR connector and solder the ground to the metal speaker chassis. Then simply connect the XLR connector to any microphone input. The speaker will function in the same manner as any other microphone, although the large mass of the coil and magnet structure won't respond well to high frequencies. On the other hand, the large cone surface will provide an excellent low-frequency sound that, when combined with a conventional close-mic setup, is impressive and powerful.

Try this same technique with larger and smaller speakers. Try using a 15-inch speaker to capture a bass guitar. Tape a piezo microphone element to a piece of half-inch foam, and then attach it to any drumhead. Try using a 45-ohm intercom speaker as a microphone. Use your imagination and build a new, exciting sound.

Combine a Kick Drum with a Low Sine Wave

If you want to build a huge and controlled kick drum sound, combine it with a low-frequency sine wave. This technique is fairly simple as long as you understand the use of external gate control.

1. On a synthesizer—preferably analog—create a simple, pure low-frequency sine wave. If you would like, tune the note to the root pitch of your production.

2. Adjust the envelope so the release is at infinity. In other words, the note holds forever without diminishing in level.

3. Patch the synthesizer through a gate/expander.

4. Place a microphone in the kick drum and aim it at the center of the drumhead to capture plenty of attack.

5. Keep the kick mic in the mix, but patch a split output from a "Y" or a patch bay mult into the external input of the gate through which the synthesizer is running.

6. Set the gate to External mode so it opens and closes in response to the miked kick drum.

7. Adjust the gate threshold so it only opens when the kick drum is struck.

8. Adjust the gate attack and release times so the sine wave blends realistically with the kick.

You can blend the sound produced by the sine wave with the kick sound perfectly on a mono track, or you can print the synth sound in stereo to separate pair of tracks to be blended during mixdown.

In addition, it is very convenient to sample the synth tone separately, layering it on the sampler with the miked kick sound. With this technique in mind, sample all 12 pitches in the low frequency range with a moderate attack and length so you'll have instant tonal support for any sampled kick drum.

Audio Example 4-4

Adding the Low Sine Wave to the Kick Drum Sample

Sampling Snare Drum

Along with the kick drum, the snare sound is fundamental in defining the sound of a mix. If it is aggressive and powerful, the song will probably sound aggressive and powerful. If it is soft and mellow, the song is likely to feel soft and mellow. The impact of the snare sound must match the emotion of the song.

Vary the Mic Distance

When tracking a complete drum kit, isolation is a fundamental consideration, so the snare mic must be close to the drumhead. During sampling, try moving the mic a foot or two away from the drumhead and use a condenser microphone instead of a moving-coil mic. You'll probably find that the snare sound is full and clean with little or no equalization.

Audio Example 4-5

Varying the Mic Distance on the Snare Drum

Multiple Microphones

Aim a microphone at the top of the snare drum to capture the full body of the sound. Aim a separate mic at the bottom of the drum to capture the crisp buzz from the rattling snares. If the room warrants it, place a mic or two at distant positions to capture the room's ambient character.

Audio Example 4-6

Miking the Top and Bottom of the Snare Drum

Layer Snare Sounds

Combine a full and low snare sound with a high and bright snare sound. Blend the sounds so they feel like they belong together.

If you find a great aggressive snare sound, try combining it with a separate sample tuned down so that it sounds very large and powerful—possibly even cumbersome. The result promises to exhibit aggression and dimension.

Additionally, layer snare drum and tom sounds to increase the breadth of the snare sound. Layering drums requires that you carefully blend the sounds so they feel like one sound. The supporting drum

Sampling Snare Drum

The sound variations offered by snare drum are vast. Each mic and each position provides a different sound. Experiment with mic placement and choice before you start processing the sound. As a rule of thumb, moving the mic toward the center of the drum provides more attack; moving the mic toward the rim provides more tone. Also, moving the mic close to the drum produces less leakage from the other drums; moving the mic farther away provides a more natural sound.

Choose a condenser coil mic for a full, natural, and clean snare sound. Choose a moving coil mic for a sound with more of an upper midrange edge.

From a relatively close distance, use the built-in pad on a condensor mic to avoid overdriving the mic circuitry and the mixer or sampler input.

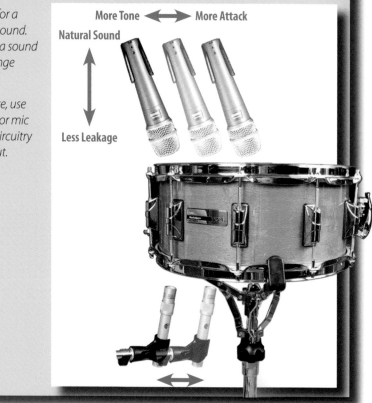

More Tone ←→ More Attack

Natural Sound

Less Leakage

is typically weak in comparison to the primary drum—often weak enough that it's difficult to hear when it's on, but obviously gone when it's muted.

Video Example 4-2

Snare Drum Sampling Techniques

Sampling Toms

Toms, in particular, need to feel present, intimate, and full in most mixes. Each musical genre and era has a sound that is typically associated with the toms. Rock of almost any type from the '70s and early '80s is defined by the single-head tom sound. Eventually everyone migrated to the double-head tom sound. Sometimes a wide-open extremely resonant tom sound works great, whereas other times a more muffled sound is more appropriate for the musical context.

Mic Choice and Position

Experiment with mic type and distance first. In close-miking the kit, moving-coil mics, such as the Shure SM 57 or Sennheiser 421, are excellent choices because they can withstand the volume produced at close proximity to the drumhead and also because they both sound fuller from close proximity (two to six inches) than they do from a greater distance.

Try sampling toms using various condenser microphones from distances of six inches to a foot or two—listen closely to the sonic differences. Much will depend on the amount of force used to strike the drum, the acoustic space, and the drum tone. Some of the best tom sounds I've found have been miked with condenser mics from about 12 to 18 inches.

Experiment with large- and small-diaphragm condenser mics. Each will typically provide a very different feel. A small-diaphragm condenser mic might provide a very transparent sound with an excellent and very noticeable transient attack. A large-diaphragm tube mic might provide a warm, full tom sound with a deep tone and a subdued attack. Many of the differences provided by mic choices can't be duplicated simply through EQ changes.

Trimming and Shaping

For sampling purposes, it's a good idea to develop a diverse catalog of many tom sounds. It's often difficult to find the perfect tom sound, especially if you have a strong musical opinion. Once you develop some excellent tom samples and have organized them properly, you'll be very thankful during production.

When tracking live drums, there are other considerations that are nearly as important as tone.

- Typically, the toms must be close-miked so there is sufficient isolation to avoid creating a distant, overly ambient sound on the entire kit.

- The toms need to be controlled or muffled in such a way that they aren't continually ringing when they're not being played.

- Often the tuning for one or more toms must be altered to avoid causing a ring or buzz from the snare drum every time a tom is struck.

Fortunately, sampling affords the luxury of considering tone and attack as the primary concerns. Whereas continuously ringing toms are an important consideration while tracking a complete drum set, any extra ring isn't really a problem when sampling because the length of the tom sound can easily be controlled through editing. Either use a volume fade or an automatic level fade to perfectly match the length of the toms to your production needs.

Once the sample is completed, keep the original version even if the tone rings excessively. Save shortened versions of the sample under the same name using a descriptive suffixes, such as _short, _shrt, 1sec, 2sec, and so on.

Video Example 4-3

Sampling the Tom

Controlling Tom Ring

The best time to control a ringing sampled tom is right after it has been recorded. Save the original sample and then save a copy that you can trim and shape. The tom waveform below lasts about four beats, which is too long in most cases. Use the volume control parameter to adjust the tom fade so it is controlled, yet natural-sounding. When you've shaped the decay, trim off the excess and upload your perfectly crafted tom sound to your sampler.

Tom2023
Original Tom Waveform

Tom2023
Controlled Decay

Trim Excess

A well-tuned tom with new heads, an excellent mount system, and superior construction and materials will almost always sound great. If the tom sound you're looking for needs to feel a bit mellow or subdued, try muffling the drum with various materials. Any substance that dampens the vibrations of the drumhead is worth trying. Although most producers and engineers prefer a tom that has great tone that isn't immediately choked, this doesn't mean you shouldn't experiment with different sounds. You might come up with the latest and greatest thing.

Muffling

A few materials are commonly used to muffle drumheads. With all muffling materials, move toward the center of the head to increase muffling and move toward the rim to decrease muffling. You should try these and more to see which type of tom sound is right for your music. Maybe you'll prefer no muffling at all. Additionally, these muffling techniques apply to the kick and snare drums.

- **Moon Gel.** This is a commercially manufactured substance that does a great job of muffling any drum. It feels and looks a little like well-set Jell-O that's about an eighth of an inch thick and roughly one-inch square. It sticks to the tom head without leaving a residue and can be easily moved to adjust the amount of dampening. The low mass, small size, and ease of placement offered by Moon Gel make it an excellent tool for muffling drums, and it provides a great tone, too.

- **Muffling ring.** The muffling ring is simply a one-inch-wide hoop cut from drumhead material, with its outer dimension the same size as the drum it is muffling. These rings lie on top of the drumhead, evenly muffling the head without completely choking the sound. They work pretty well in most cases.

+ **Duct tape.** Duct tape is often used to dampen drums. It really does a pretty poor job as a muffling material. It leaves an ugly, sticky residue and it produces a muffled sound that is dated, lacking in warmth and pure tone.

+ **Weather stripping.** Weather stripping is an excellent muffling tool. It can be torn off in whichever length provides the perfect tone, and its density is often just right for a great tom sound. The only problem with weather stripping is that it leaves a sticky residue much like duct tape.

Try these techniques, as well as the techniques outlined in *The S.M.A.R.T. Guide to Recording Great Tracks in a Small Studio.* You'll find that they all provide unique tom sounds. Some will be very usable on your projects, while others won't.

Sampling Cymbals

In most sampling synthesizers, the included cymbal samplers are questionable. They're often fairly short because the manufacturer is trying to save memory for other sounds. Nothing gives away an amateur production quite like a short, dull cymbal sample.

Cymbal samples typically sound best when miked from at least a couple feet away. The problem with close-miking any cymbal is the phase interaction between the mic and the cymbal as the cymbal moves in response to being struck.

Crash

Sample crash cymbals using a stereo X-Y technique to add a natural space to the sound. If you're building a group of cymbals that will be used together in a set, set them up in their normal positions and then sample each cymbal, including the ride cymbal, from the same coincident stereo or surround microphone setup. This will help build a realistic stereo image for the drum kit.

For an interesting effect, try miking the cymbals from underneath with the mic aimed up at the bell of the cymbal. Keep in mind that the

Miking Cymbals

Given that you have cymbals that sound good, and that the acoustic environment is acceptable, there are two main considerations in sampling cymbals:

1.   The microphone's distance from the cymbal

2.   The mic posistion in relation to the bell and edge of the cymbal

The mic should be at least two feet from the cymbal. If it is too close, a phase-shifting effect is produced when the cymbal moves in response to being struck. As the cymbal (especially a crash cymbal) moves, reflections between the close mic and cymbal sweep through a range of changing cancellations and summing, resulting in a rapidly sweeping flanger or phase-shifter sound.

Additionally, aim the mic at the cymbal's bell to capture more high frequencies, or point the mic at the edge to capture low frequencies.

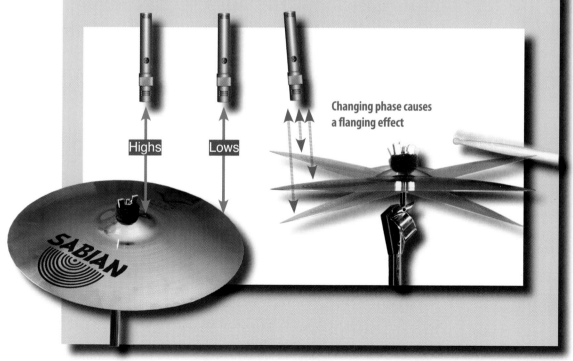

Highs   **Lows**   **Changing phase causes a flanging effect**

high frequencies emanate from the bell and the low-frequency gong-like sounds come from the outer edge of the cymbal.

Ride

The ride cymbal typically contains more of a ping sound than the crashes. Sometimes it's appropriate to place a separate mic close to the ride cymbal to help define the cutting sound of the stick attack on the cymbal.

Audio Example 4-7

Sampling Cymbals

Special Effects

Try sampling using special delay and reverberation effects. If you want samples that are quick and easy to use in a live application, it might be a good idea to include effects in the actual sample. However, in most instances it's best to use the onboard effects provided in your hardware or software sampler or to simply wait until mixdown to apply effects selected specifically for the feeling of the mix.

Mallets and Other Types of Sticks

Once you've sampled sounds of drums or cymbals being struck with regular drumsticks, try striking the instruments with other types of sticks. Whereas heavy drumsticks produce a sound that is different from light sticks, each other type of striking device produces a unique sound. Use these different types of sticks on cymbals and/or toms to build a unique and interesting drum sample catalog. Use your imagination.

+ Felt-tip mallets
+ Wool-tip mallets
+ Plastic-tip sticks
+ Wood-tip sticks

- ✦ Metal sticks
- ✦ Triangle beater
- ✦ Phillips screwdriver
- ✦ Plastic or metal coat hangers

Achieve a Live, Ambient Feel

Often an entire drum kit made up completely from sampled drums produces an overall sound that lacks a natural blend. Reverberation effects can help blend the sounds, but they don't always provide a natural ambient feel like a real drum kit does.

Part of what is missing when you use sampled drum sounds to make up the full kit is the leakage between microphones, as well as the reflections from the acoustic surfaces in the room. To help the samples feel more real and authentic, place a high-quality pair of speakers in a room that would normally record drums and then set up a stereo or surround microphone configuration. Move the mics and speakers to different room locations to hear how the sound is affected. Once you find the best-sounding combination of locations, play the drum tracks over the speakers and record them through the room microphones onto a separate set of tracks. Blend these room tracks in lightly with the samples and listen to how the drums blend together into a more authentic sound.

Replacing Drum Sounds

Depending on the genre, many of the drum sounds heard in hit recordings were never part of the original kit. Even though it's apparent that the drums were recorded in the studio and played by a real person as the drum track specifically for the song in which they're heard, very few of the drums may be from the original tracking session.

It is very common in pop, country, and rock production to replace the toms, snare, and kick with other more impressive sounds. Many sampled drum sounds would be difficult, if not impossible, to record in the basic tracking session. However, often these sampled drums sound larger than life—they're huge and impressive. So the temptation to replace the original smaller-sounding drum sounds with the "drums on steroids" is irresistible.

Hardware Audio-to-MIDI Converter

To accomplish drum replacement, you need a device (hardware or software) that responds to audio input by producing a MIDI note. Simply patch the output of the audio drum channel into the input of a MIDI trigger device, and then record the MIDI signals into your sequencer. Once you have captured the MIDI data, assign the MIDI track to trigger your sampled sounds.

The most important factor in achieving successful MIDI data from an audio signal is the adjustment of the threshold. Every signal that surpasses the threshold will produce a MIDI note, so careful adjustment is critical. This procedure always works best when the track contains audio from a single drum because the unwanted leakage can be filtered out more easily.

Use the technology at hand. If you're playing the audio from your digital recording software or through a mixer with automation, isolate specific hits—turn the rest of the track down or off until the drum you want is played. Turn the desired track on and up to send a signal to trigger a MIDI note, and then turn it off again. This procedure works well for toms, especially when the fills are pretty simple.

Keep It Simple

If you're working with the snare track, the sheer repetition causes the need for a different technique. One mark of an excellent drummer is the ability to play a solid part that is focused and to the point. Many young drummers play a lot of extra notes. Their fills are often too complex and they do more to destroy the musicality of the song than they do to enhance it. Once you start triggering MIDI notes from recorded drums you will definitely appreciate the beauty of simplicity.

If your snare track is simple and authoritative, triggering is much easier. If the drummer has a light left hand and a passive feel, you're probably in big trouble all the way around—and this is not to mention triggering MIDI notes.

Considering that the snare track is clean and punchy, there still might be a little too much leakage to get a clean MIDI track.

Filtering

Try patching the original snare through an equalizer. Adjust the equalizer by ear so that the drum you want is by far the loudest thing on the track. Filter out the low frequencies to minimize kick leakage. Filter out the high frequencies to minimize cymbal leakage. Zero in on the exact frequency range that contains the body of the drum sound, and boost that frequency. Once you've gotten rid of as much unwanted sound as possible and once the leakage has been minimized, patch the equalizer output into the audio-to-MIDI trigger input. This should help strengthen the MIDI signals.

Editing MIDI Data

Once the MIDI data has been successfully recorded into your sequencer, you'll probably need to edit the note data to create a track that fits seamlessly into the original drum track. Typically, at least the cymbal mics (overheads, rides, and hi-hats) are kept in their original state to help the drums maintain a realistic feel. Therefore, any drum replacement must match the original drum placement in order to avoid flams between the original and the sample.

Often, the MIDI trigger captures erroneous data, causing false MIDI data. This is easily removed in the MIDI domain. Simply listen to the original track and erase the extra MIDI data. This process is easy and fast.

Once the MIDI data matches the original drum placements throughout the song, you have a couple obvious options.

1. Play the samples from the MIDI domain all the way through mixdown.

2. Record the samples to an audio track as they are played from the MIDI trigger.

The first option is acceptable as long as the triggered samples are perfectly in sync with the original drums, but that doesn't really happen very often. At the very least, the entire track will need to be shifted earlier to compensate for the delay time involved in the MIDI data flow.

The second option provides for the most detailed placement of the samples. As the samples are recorded to an audio track, it is very easy to tell whether the sounds line up with the original drums. Position the sample audio track directly below the original track and zoom in to see graphically exactly how the notes line up. If they don't line up perfectly, simply move the sample into place. If a trigger was missed, copy and paste the sample into the proper position.

Video Example 4-4

Replacing a Drum Sound

Percussion and Sampling

Percussion sampling is in many ways identical to sampling the drum set instruments. As with the other drums, once you're set to sample any percussion instrument, consider all the possible sounds that can be created from that instrument. If you're sampling a tambourine with a head, all of these sounds should be sampled in case they're needed in the future.

- Hitting the left palm with the tambourine held by the right hand
- Hitting the head with the palm
- Hitting the head with a closed fist
- Hitting the rim with the tambourine held vertically
- Hitting the rim with the tambourine held horizontally
- Tapping the rim of a horizontal tambourine
- Hitting the rim with a drumstick
- Hitting the head with a drumstick
- Playing the tambourine in eight notes fast, medium, and slow

It could be that you only need a simple tambourine hit to augment the snare drum on counts two and four; however, you might need more than you have predicted once the track is laid down.

When you're on your own time, always record as many samples as you can think of. Of course, if you're in the middle of a paid session, only record as many as the client is comfortable with.

In-Tempo Percussion Grooves

While you're sampling anyway, record several basic rhythm patterns with each percussion instrument. Set up a pattern on a drum machine or play along with a prerecorded groove to make sure your percussion grooves are in time.

Keep track of reference drum patterns, and as you sample, play along with each of your references until you're certain that you've captured a great-feeling rhythmic performance.

Sampling Guitars

Nuance shapes the sound of any guitar. Whether you're recording electric or acoustic guitar, always consider the idiomatic performance characteristics of the instrument. Acoustic guitars make frequent use of choked strums—they help keep track of the groove while they open up the harmonic texture. String squeaks add realism and authenticity to any guitar part. As you're sampling guitar listen for the fine details of a great performance. Sample these sounds as well as sustained notes, chords, and strum patterns.

Electric Guitar

Guitar, like piano and most stringed instruments, produces a sound that is identified and shaped by several characteristics, such as attack, natural decay, strum speed, harmonic voicing, pitch bends, slides, hammer-ons, pick material, and so on.

Sampling a guitar for a realistic feel in the mix is far more than simply sampling one note and looping a waveform to create a long tone—it is much more involved than that. Often, a guitar part is sampled specifically to become a part of the song. The comp pattern used in the verse might be constant—it just doesn't change throughout all verses. In this case, a sample of the stereo guitar part as it is played perfectly one time through can easily provide an extremely solid foundation for any rhythm section arrangement.

Keep sampled guitar parts clean and simple. You can always layer 20 power chords over the top later if you must.

Rhythmic Comp Loops

Many rhythmic comp licks are recorded specifically for one song. To get more use out of your sampling time, record the comp at various tempos and in various keys. Most digital recording programs are very good at time compression and expansion, so increasing and decreasing speed isn't typically much of a problem. However, altering the pitch of a harmonic comp (one that contains a lot of full chords) is difficult. It often doesn't work at all and is only sometimes passable. Hence, it's a good idea to record the comp in all of the primary keys that you think might possibly work well in your productions.

Additionally, if you're trying to create authentic realistic guitar parts, you'll need to play in the correct key and in the correct range. Simply play the comps adjusted to work well in each key. You'll probably find much use for them in the future, especially considering how easy it is to cut and paste the audio. Forming new, fresh guitar parts from two or three previously used segments is not only easy, it's pretty fun too.

Create Multichannel Sound

Experiment with multiple mic techniques. Set up a stereo room mic configuration to increase the size of the sound. Blend these room mics with the direct mics to create the perfect sound; however, be conservative in the amount of room sound you include. If you create a sound that is distant, lacking intimacy, you might be disappointed during mixdown.

The most efficient way to create multichannel sounds includes the DAW. Set up several mics, including multiple stereo setups, close mics aimed at both the center and outer edge of the speaker, and mics placed between three and eight feet from the speaker cabinet. As the loop or sample is performed, record each mic to a separate track. On playback, mix several combinations of the loop, ranging from the most intimate-sounding close mic to the most ambient-sounding stereo or surround configuration.

Multitrack Guitar Loops

Set up several mics on the guitar cabinet. Record each mic to a separate track and then mix several versions of the same loop or sample. This procedure provides flexibility in the creative process.

Personally, I prefer a simplistic approach when tracking guitars with a band. I'd rather find the mic and position that provides a great sound, which can be blended into the mix, than use several mics and build a sound that might be disastrous during mixdown.

Recording for samples and loops, however, is the perfect place to take chances. As long as you're able to mix several versions of the same performance, saving each version for playback at a later time, you maintain creative freedom in the production process. It is also very likely that different versions of the same loop performance might work perfectly well in different parts of the production.

Increase the scope of your multichannel samples by including multiple amplifiers. Numbers 1 – 6 indicate mic positions, and number 7 indicates a direct feed to the mixer. The direct signal can be processed by one of the excellent available plug-ins or recorded direct to blend with the microphones.

Augment this multichannel approach by including multiple amplifiers and an excellent direct box—use a signal splitter to maintain signal integrity. Many great guitar sounds can be found in the multiple amplifier approach.

Varying Multisamples across the Keyboard

Try playing variations of the rhythmic and melodic comps, sampling each to a new key on the MIDI keyboard. This is a simple way to build a guitar part along with the song by switching notes to trigger variations. In addition, using this technique, it's no problem to chain patterns together or to save separate samples of the first and last halves of all of the patterns. This makes it very easy to switch from the first half of pattern one to the second half of pattern two, and so on.

Video Example 4-5

Sampling Electric Guitar with Multiple Mics

Acoustic Guitar

Acoustic guitar parts consist of many textures and lots of idiomatically expressive and unique elements. To record usable acoustic guitar samples, you must include the unique sounds of different strum and plucking techniques. The rhythmic comp consists of almost as many rhythmic chucks and ghosted notes as it does clean and clear tones.

Choose a rhythmic comp pattern. Record the entire pattern and divide it up into all of the unique sounds that you can find—you'll probably be surprised at the number of sounds. Separate them out and save them as unique samples. Once they're listed and arranged you'll be able to use them as separate ingredients to construct new guitar patterns.

Multisamples and Acoustic Guitar

Guitar samples are similar to piano samples in that even if they can be tuned to a degree, they sound unnatural if they're tuned too far in either direction. Therefore, whenever you are sampling single notes, it's advisable to sample several different notes throughout the range of the instrument. At the very least, you should sample each open string.

The same theory applies to sampling comps, licks, and riffs: Perform the part in all possible keys for your production and assign each to a different note on the MIDI keyboard.

Combining Acoustic Guitar Sounds

Use your creativity to build unique acoustic sounds. Use a capo on any guitar to change the timbre. As the strings are shortened, the open strings rise in pitch and the harmonic interactions change, providing a unique timbre.

Sample the strum of a chord in open position and then sample a similar strum of a higher voicing. Layer these two samples in stereo to create a larger-than-life sound.

Most usable acoustic guitar samples consist of strum patterns that last one or two measures. If you're developing for multiple projects, record two measures of several diatonic chords. A diatonic chord is made up from notes stacked in thirds that exist in the tonic scale. For example, in the key of D the naturally occurring triads are D, Em, F#m, G, A, Bm, C#dim. The naturally occurring four-note chords are Dmaj7, Em7, F#m7, Gmaj7, A7, Bm7, C#m7(−5).

Once you've sampled strum patterns, simply mix and match the chords to come up with excellent chord progression options.

Video Example 4-6

Acoustic Guitar Multisamples

Sampling the Bass Guitar

Bass guitar, like electric and acoustic guitars, contains many other sounds in a performance than only simple bass tones. String squeaks, glissandos, slaps, thumps, hammer-ons, pull-offs, and string snaps all provide the realism that makes a bass guitar part authentic.

To build a comprehensive sample library, record an excellent bassist playing an excellent bass part and then isolate the nuance and idiomatic sounds, saving each as a separate sample. Keep the label name from the original sample, identifying the specific sounds using a descriptive suffix, such as _squeak, _snap, _hammer. _pulloff, and so on.

Sample multiple notes throughout the bass range. At least sample the open strings; however, keep in mind that there is a difference between the timbre of open strings and fretted notes. Most bass parts consist primarily of fretted notes, so it's a good idea to sample several fretted notes in addition to open strings.

Video Example 4-7

Bass Guitar Multisamples

Movie Soundtrack Samples

The first time you produce music and sound design for a film or dramatic video, you'll understand the true value of sound in picture. A mediocre visual can be transformed into a powerful scene when supported by perfect sounds and music. On the other hand, a first-class scene can easily be cheapened by inappropriate sound design and music.

Supporting visuals with audio requires access to myriad natural sounds. The picture inspires the specific need, but as you develop your library in preparation for your upcoming film project, listen to the sounds around you in various real-life settings. Eventually, you will probably need the sounds of computer keys tapping, fans running in the background, radio shows, television programs, babies crying, footsteps, and so on.

Portable laptop-based systems are perfect tools to facilitate your sampling needs for sound effects and location recording. There a few excellent choices to help you capture field audio and sampled effects. If you're recording stereo samples, check out the Digidesign Mbox. It offers two phantom-powered microphone preamps and multiple monitoring options, all in a very compact package. In addition, the Mbox is completely powered by the computer through the USB connection. Systems like this free you to record high-quality audio virtually anywhere.

Once you have a respectable library of animal sounds, screams, yells, baseballs being caught, balls being hit, and so on, try layering them behind your musical samples. Often, these sounds help provide an emotion for the music that wouldn't otherwise exist. Even if sounds are virtually inaudible they will probably change the feel of the music.

When sound effects inspired by visuals are added to supporting music, the emotional impact of the entire film benefits dramatically.

Vocal Samples

Most of you who own synthesizers that manipulate sampled audio have experienced a bank of human vocal sounds. After the first time you hear them they become less appealing. The last sounds most producers want to include in their music are sounds that anyone with the keyboard of the day will recognize as stock in the basic keyboard library. Therefore, these stock vocal sounds are of little value other than to impress a potential buyer on the showroom floor.

On the other hand, custom vocal sounds and human beatbox grooves are often very useful in production. Depending on the genre, custom vocal sounds add personality and character that is specific to a production.

Oohs, Ahs, and Ohs

If your music lends itself to vocal pads consisting of oohs, ahs, and ohs, build an impressive sound by sampling vocalists. Within your digital recording software, overdub several vocal layers and then combine them to a stereo track.

Build a series of unison and octave pads of each syllable you want to use. This might take a while, but it will provide a sound that is unique to your productions. Layer several tracks of your singer or singers singing one note. Pan them across the stereo or surround panorama, and then sample the entire group. If you sample several notes in the usable pitch range, you'll be able to perform long unison passages or you can simply play chords to build a harmonic group.

It also works very well to sample singers performing an octave interval. One very usable sound for backing vocals takes advantage of men and women singing the identical musical line an octave apart.

Lengthening the Vocal Pad

Vocal pads are typically held anywhere from a half of a measure to several measures. It would be impractical to record multiple lengths of these tones, so looping a waveform or group of waveforms is necessary. Set a length that provides indiscernible loop points, and then set the release so it sounds naturally smooth.

Vocal Licks

Often, the out choruses are embellished by vocal improvisation. A sampler can be very valuable in this context because it is so easy to cut up an overdubbed track, assigning each lick or part of a lick to a different key. This process provides a simple way to test the licks in the different song sections.

Once you have sampled each lick, assign it to a single key on the MIDI keyboard. Locate the samples from the lowest keyboard notes and add each new sample to the next available key. This way, it's easy to keep track of a sequence of licks throughout a production.

Using Loops

Loops are in common use today. The recording industry, at every level, has embraced loops as a viable creative tool. The purist would rather have a real drummer playing real drums—I have to admit that I fit into that category for most productions. On the other hand, the solid rhythmic feel and creative ease-of-use provided by excellent samples and loops is often irresistible.

Definition of Loops

In its simplest form, a loop is a digital recording designed to be played over and over continuously until a variation or change is appropriate. Loops most commonly consist of drum or percussion grooves. The early popularity of grooves grew because these real drum recordings strung together in the proper order sounded and felt just like a good recording of a great drummer. Young recordists who had no access to world-class players, microphones, preamps, effects, and mixers could build a world-class foundation for their compositions and productions.

In addition to drum and percussion grooves, loops of other instruments soon became popular. Guitar, bass, synth, and vocal loops provided textural and creative options that helped extend the capacity of under-equipped recordists. Typically, a genre that demonstrates extensive use of loops from all instruments tends to become increasingly mono-tonal. Although this doesn't have to be the case because most loop performance software provides for modulation of pitch-instrument loops, music that relies on loops tends to focus creativity on other creative ingredients, such as the groove, textural changes, rhythmic breakdowns, vocal riffs, spoken lyrics, and harmonically simple melodies.

Common Lengths of Loops

Any recording used specifically for loop playback should fit into a standard musical phrase. Typically, loops should be one, two, four, or eight measures to fit evenly into a standard verse, chorus, or bridge. Most musical sections are four, eight, or 12 measures long.

The majority of popular songs consist of four-beat measures. Some modern songs consist of three-beat measures. Depending on your musical needs and the tonal structure, it sometimes provides a unique feeling to layer a group of three-beat measures over a groove consisting of four beats per measure.

A three-beat pattern that repeats itself four times to end up back in sync on beat one can help provide compelling rhythmic interest. As the phrase repeats itself, it doesn't seem to simply loop quite as much as an even number of beats or measures. Patterns like this are particularly useful in a production that is rather mono-tonal. In trance and many techno recordings, there is little harmonic structure change, so a pattern that creates interest without dramatically altering tonality is very useful.

Loop Length

Most loops fit evenly into common eight-bar musical phrases. One-, two-, four-, and eight-bar phrases provide a solid rhythmic pattern and conform to standard musical form. Many loops are recorded to mimic the flow of a popular commercial song, sometimes labelling variations according to musical sections such as verse, chorus, and bridge.

1-Bar Phrase	**2-Bar Phrase**
4-Bar Phrase	
8-Bar Phrase	

Chaining phrases together in varying order maintains the musical structure while creating subtle variations similar to a live musical performance.

Combined Phrases — Four 1-Bar Phrases / Two 2-Bar Phrases
1-Bar Phrase — Two 4-Bar Phrases
Verse
Chorus
Bridge
3-Bar Phrases — Four 3-Bar Phrases

Building a Track Using Loops

An amazing number of hit recordings utilize loops. The fact that loops are typically digital recordings of authentic instruments lends them to producing realistic and powerful music. The most powerful uses of loops are based on decisions to intentionally create the kind of track that takes advantage of the repetitive, sometimes trance-like feeling that loops often provide. The least effective use of loops is typically the result of a copout, where a real drummer would create much more life for the musical need, but the loop is used because it's easier. A musical decision to include the tools perfect for the song is always more emotionally powerful than a desire for speed and simplicity.

Software Choices for Mac and Windows

Loops have become so popular that it's relatively easy to find excellent software capable of playing loops, adjusting tempos and speeds, and piecing the loops together into a well-constructed piece of music. The problem is not in the software, it's in expressing focused creativity using a very unconventional music toolset.

Macintosh Software

The obvious recommendation for basic Mac loop manipulation software is GarageBand. This application brought the musical organization of loops to the masses. Anyone with a Mac and a little bit of creativity could put together a song using high-quality, well-thought-out loops. Tempo and key are variable, and instrumental tracks can be adjusted to follow a user-determined chord progression.

Although GarageBand is by no means a power-user tool, it is a very efficient application. It's an excellent songwriting tool and it's very easy to use. With little to no training, you should be able to get this program up, running, and functional in every way.

Additionally, there are excellent plug-ins from Mark of the Unicorn, Native-Instruments, Big Fish Audio, Steinberg, Propellerhead, Spectrasonics, eLab, and others that can turn your Mac into an incredible loop machine. Using loop manipulation plug-ins along with your digital recording software is the most powerful and flexible way to work with loops. The immediacy of recording audio along with MIDI while supporting the entire production through the use of prerecorded loops is very efficient, convenient, and creatively freeing.

Windows Software

As a Mac user, I was enticed into the Windows world by Sonic Foundry's Acid. Now owned by Sony Media Software, this application popularized the incorporation of loops into commercial music. Acid provided great-sounding drum and percussion loops controlled by a software architecture that provided for easy tempo and pitch changes. They have continued to provide excellent creative options for Windows users.

There are several other programs that help control loop playback on the PC, such as Fruityloops, Reason, HALion, and Kontakt.

Additionally, there are several excellent plug-ins that run on top of your digital recording software. With these plug-ins, loop tempos adjust to the sequence tempo—everything fits together seamlessly. This is a perfect example of where a strong relationship with a professional retail expert is crucial. It is their job to keep up on the newest and best tools.

Using Loops in Your Digital Recording System

The most efficient means of incorporating loops into your creative process utilizes plug-ins, which organize and access a library of great-sounding loops. Record your audio and MIDI tracks as you normally would, and then access your loops as you would any other virtual instrument. Select loops and grooves from the associated plug-in library, and they'll follow along with the sequence tempo automatically and perfectly in sync.

In conjunction with your DAW software, the loop instrument responds to MIDI commands and provides an environment where excellent musical inspiration can quickly and easily turn into excellent music.

Importing Loops into the DAW

Although cumbersome at times, depending on your recording software most modern applications easily import loops from almost any format or library. Importing generic loops is convenient in that it brings the loop ingredients into a familiar working environment. But it can also be a bit cumbersome. Single loops can be set to loop for specified numbers of measures within the DAW software. This process is workable, although it's not typically as user-friendly as working within the loop management plug-ins.

Most applications contain a window that lists all of the audio ingredients in a project, as well as provide sample and bit-rate conversions where appropriate, either manually or automatically. When you're importing loops, this is typically the proper window for accessing the loops from the CD or DVD containing the data.

When the loops are importing, set your DAW preferences so that the incoming audio is automatically adjusted to match the bit and sample rates of the rest of the audio. Typically, if the loops don't match the resolution of previously recorded audio, they won't play back. They might look like they're functional, but you won't hear them until you convert them to match the project resolution.

Define the BPM for the Loop Tempo Map

It's important that you ascertain the original tempo of any loops you import into your project. It is best if the audio loops are tagged with the beats per minute at which the original recordings were performed. Once the loop is associated with a specific tempo, it is a simple matter to fit the loop to a new tempo. Simply locate the menu item that adjusts the loop (sound bite) to the sequence tempo. Through this selection, it's a simple matter to match the tempo of the loop to the sequence tempo, even when you make minor changes in the final stages of production.

BPM Tags on Loops

Since loops contain measures with multiple beats, there must be a way to control their tempo in order to use them with your custom music. Professional loop libraries contain tempo information which is typically interpreted by a DAW or sampler. The illustration below demonstrates the documentation from the Big Fish Audio "LA Drum Sessions" library. Notice the BPM column makes the original loop tempo perfectly clear.

Even though most software-based systems are capable of converting audio between any tempos, it is still valuable to know the original tempo; if the original tempo is dramatically different than your production, conversion accuracy is questionable.

bigfishaudio™
professional sound libraries

LA Drum Sessions

CD-ROM CONTENTS:

Folder	BPM	Loops
Disc I		
'50s (3-4 time)	180	96
'60s	132	63
'60s Fun	115	156
Blues (Chicago)	120	117
Blues (slow)	80	87
Blues	88	153
Boom Boom	150	96
Country Shuffle	160	84
Country Waltz	134	96
Disco	125	126
Fast 'N Furious	140	135
Fast Rock	170	159
Faster Rock	250	120
Funk	84	72
Funky	110	99

Loop Library Sources

Loops are readily available. The Internet is an excellent source of loop libraries. Simply open your favorite search engine and perform a search for the type of loop you need: drum loop, bass loop, guitar loop, and so on. Several free loops are available, although typically the best and most musically powerful loops are contained in high-quality, highly respected, fee-based libraries.

The most efficient and productive creative environment combines excellent loop libraries with excellent organizational structure. When you're producing music under a tight schedule, yet you want to take advantage of the incredible array of available technology, the organizational simplicity of plug-ins, such as MOTU's Mach 5, Native-Instruments' Kontakt, or Spectrasonics' Stylus RMX, or eLab's Foundation offers incredible value.

The convenience and functionality of a large list of loops that are brilliantly organized and field tested before you even get your hands on them provides a tool for you to do more creating and less searching for the right groove. Even when they're organized well, the sheer number

Loop Libraries

There are many libraries available and there are many that are just plain excellent. Companies like Native Instruments, Big Fish Audio, and Spectrasonics are representative of excellent companies that are providing amazing-sounding loops and samples. Additionally, the libraries included with most virtual samplers like Mach 5, Kontakt, Foundation, Stylus RMX, Trilogy, and Atmosphere are exceptional.

of loops in a working library presents you with the daunting task of locating the perfect groove for your musical setting. The emotion and feeling of a musical production is immensely important, so it's crucial that your library of loops and sounds is comprehensive enough to afford you sufficient creative options.

Video Example 5-1

Importing Loops into the Digital Audio Workstation

Multitrack Loops

Most loops are available in stereo. However, there are some wonderful drum loops available in multitrack format, with the kick drum, snare drum, toms, overheads, and hi-hat spread out across eight tracks. Multitrack loops like these let the user control the mix all the way through the end of the production. Frequently during mixdown, the orchestration changes to create a textural interest that compels the listener. This often includes either muting the drum tracks or thinning the drum track down until there is only a kick drum, or maybe a kick and hi-hat. Multitrack loops provide constant flexibility to create the optimum musical flow.

It has also become more common to see surround loops consisting of six or eight tracks for providing 5.1 or 7.1 surround-sound imaging. These surround images are typically very high quality and often are delivered in high-resolution audio formats.

The Groove

When you're selecting loops to work together musically, you must evaluate them on a few levels.

+ Do they have the same or compatible meters?

+ Are they compatible texturally?

+ Do the fall into the same groove?

Of these considerations, it's most important that the loops all possess the same groove. If the primary groove feels laid back, the rest of the loops either need to feel laid back or they must adjust the groove in a calculated and musically intelligent manner. Sometimes it's a good idea to use a groove that is a little less relaxed for the chorus, but it's not typically effective to randomly change the feel throughout the song just because the perfect loop didn't immediately reveal itself.

The process involved in creating an excellent song structure using loops can be very time-consuming—often it feels almost as time-consuming as tracking real drums. You must be diligent in finding loops that provide the solid foundation your music deserves.

Creating a Bed

The foundation for most popular commercial songs comes from the drum track. As you begin to build your foundation using loops, search through your library until you locate a loop with just the right feel. Because most loops are simply audio recordings of real performances, you must realize that with each performance comes the musician's groove tendency. Some players find the groove behind the beat, while others find it on top of or ahead of the beat. When loops are strung together, it feels uncomfortable when the groove tendency changes abruptly.

Most libraries group a loop with several versions of the same loop. With the same drummer performing variations, the feel is usually very consistent between loops. When building your foundation for any song, take advantage of the patterns that have been grouped together—they'll provide the same feel and the same drums, and they're convenient.

If you need to use loops from a different family, be sure the feels match. The only way to verify that loops flow well together is to set up a track where the loops in question play together. Be sure you check them in any possible combination. It must feel musical no matter how the loops are arranged.

Audio Example 5-1

Different Grooves at a Constant Tempo

Layering

Once the rhythmic foundation has been established, consider the textural arrangement. It's a good idea to add the bass guitar part next to help establish the form and tonality. Once the basic grooves are in place, the bass guitar part can be constructed to fit with the kick and snare patterns. It's almost always a good idea to build the bass guitar so that it matches or complements the fundamental rhythms of the kick drum. Rhythmic punches and anticipations that match the kick-drum pattern provide momentum and polish.

Once the bass and drums are established, consider layering percussion loops over the main groove track. Percussion loops vary dramatically in texture. Some very simple loops contain a single instrument playing a simple rhythm; other percussion loops contain an entire ensemble playing nearly every percussion instrument ever made. Your decisions must be based on musical needs. Sometimes a loop sounds great all alone, but once it's in the track with the other instruments, it's far too busy. With a substantial library at hand you can always add more percussion tracks, so add ingredients sparingly.

The goal should be to build the musical sections, creating contrast and emotional flow.

Once you've layered the percussion parts over the fundamental groove and the bass guitar is functional, construct the harmonic bed. If you're using loops for the harmonic foundation, be sure you've defined

Layering Loops

Since loops from commercial libraries are, by nature, available to the public, it's important to customize them in some way—layering them with other rhythm and percussion ingredients is a very convenient way to help them feel like they were made just for your production.

There are a few very effective ways to customize your grooves:

- *Layer a live percussion track along with the groove.*
- *Layer additional loops over your basic pattern.*
- *Layer a MIDI pattern over the audio loop.*

Virtual samplers and loop software provide simple architecture for layering audio loops; some even provide virtual effects racks to help sonically mold the loop to fit your production. The Stylus RMX screen below demonstrates layers and effects working together to create a custom sound from standard ingredients.

the key. Most harmonic loops indicate their original key, which provides a couple functions.

✦ It indicates the key of the original recording.

✦ It helps provide intelligent options for transposing the loops to support the harmonic structure.

When the rhythmic and harmonic structures have been adequately defined, record a reference vocal. Whether in a traditional or rap genre, this reference vocal is a very important part of the production process. Quite often, the reference vocal contains the most life and raw emotion of all the takes. Always save the reference vocal track—it might be the take you use in the final mix.

Build the remaining tracks according to the breaks in the vocal track. Listen to the arrangement and determine whether the drums and percussion loops are too busy or whether you need more rhythmic support for certain musical sections. Base further additions on supporting the vocal track. Almost every genre depends on the melody and the primary vocal sound and delivery, so keep the focus on the lead vocal.

MIDI Loops

Not all loops are digital recordings of instrumental or vocal performances. MIDI loops are constructed of MIDI notes triggering sound modules, synthesizers, or samplers. The advantage of MIDI loops is realized through the ease of replacing sounds within the loop. Because the MIDI loop contains a rhythmic arrangement of MIDI note values rather than a digital recording, MIDI loops are very flexible.

The disadvantage of the MIDI loop lies in the likelihood that the sounds, although often samples, will not blend together into the authentic sound of the loop of a real instrumental or vocal performance.

MIDI loops are frequently the basis of techno and trance music because of the broad range of sounds and textures that can be quickly and efficiently combined. Any genre that is built on unique and unnatural or supernatural sounds is likely to benefit from the inclusion of some type of MIDI loop.

One of the tricks commonly used in the MIDI domain is to keep the groove rhythm constant while simply changing the instruments assigned to each note value. This procedure is easy to accomplish through the use of MIDI loops. On the other hand, it's impractical through the use of typical audio loops.

Supporting Video and Film with Loops

Loops are very supportive of visual images, whether film, video, or slides. An excellent percussion groove helps provide emotion, power, and passion. As you blend the music with the location audio and voiceover, be sure that the narration and dialogue are at the front of the mix and that they're consistently easy to hear and understand.

Capturing the Emotion of Visuals

Watch the images and focus on the feeling and mood produced by the images, the pacing, and the content of the voiceover. Write down your impressions and note the time of each change in mood. Most film and video productions flow smoothly throughout the emotional range. If the opening scenes are intense and fast-paced, there's a good chance that the next section will slow down to a comfortable (although somewhat

aggressive) feel. It's also likely tha emotional, floaty, and passionate s and fast-paced section.

It's fairly obvious when the moo must match the emotional changes i section change and construct loops feeling. Tempo changes are excellen Switching from a fast, aggressive g creates an appropriate feel change. Te also provide excellent visual suppor complex loop to a loop of a single inst melody creates an extreme contrast tha many scenes. Pitch changes create d from a medium percussion loop with frequency range to a slower majestic loc low-frequency percussion instruments as well as a dramatic contrast in emotic

Completing the Sound

Once the basic rhythm tracks are in pla the image, try recording a melodic instrum thing. An accomplished instrumentalist film or video and provide excellent melodi from the heart, so matching a visual impr becomes second nature.

This is the perfect setting for incorpora loop instrument because it's a simple task along with the loops. In addition, some loc as GarageBand and Acid, provide for recordi the loops.

Building Custom Loops

Loops provide a powerful production tool. Prerecorded loops are typically very useful and they sound good; however, if you want your music to take on more of your own personality, develop your own library of custom loops. A custom loop is simply a loop created for a specific purpose from stock sounds or your own personal libraries of samples and sounds. Build unique sounds and develop meticulous grooves. Record all loops, paying the closest possible attention to sound quality, shaping each loop to suit your personal musical pleasure.

Drum and percussion loops are typically built in one of two ways.

+ From separate sounds and samples sequenced through MIDI into a groove

+ From a complete recording of a drum or percussion kit, edited into one-, two-, four-, or eight-bar segments that sound continuous when they're looped

Building a Loop from Sampled and Synthesized Sounds

Building a loop from samples and synthesized sounds requires the use of a MIDI sequencer. Modern sequencing software provides ample control over each MIDI note to create a groove that feels just right.

In the MIDI-sequencing domain, you can use any available sound to create the loop. Often it's thought that loops are only sampled instruments. In actuality a loop is merely a musical segment of audio that can be played repeatedly, sounding like a continuous musical pattern.

The sounds that you developed in the sampling exercises are excellent choices to use when creating custom loops. The custom sounds provide a unique and fresh character that is different from common loop libraries.

Background Unit

Any time you build a loop or any other kind of drum or percussion pattern, decide on the background unit first. The background unit is simply the fundamental unit that defines the basic rhythmic grid. If a groove is based on sixteenth notes, where the hi-hat, ride cymbal, or other constant ingredient primarily plays sixteenth notes, then the background unit is sixteenth notes.

Funky grooves and many slow ballad grooves are often based on a sixteenth-note background unit. Straight-ahead rock grooves, in which the hi-hat plays straight eighth notes, have eighth-note background units. Swing grooves, shuffle grooves, and slow 12/8 and 6/8 ballads have an eighth-note triplet background unit.

Even if you don't end up with any instrument constantly playing it, it's a good idea (especially if you're inexperienced at creating grooves) to start with a hi-hat or shaker playing the background unit rhythm.

The Rhythmic Background Unit

The background unit is the fundamental and most basic note value in a groove or other rhythmic musical passage. It is usually understood as a continuous rhythmic flow of the underlying and continuous stream of notes containing the shortest value, not counting grace notes, ruffs, and presses. In other words, if the fastest note in the groove is a sixteenth note, then sixteenth notes provide the background unit.

Eighth Note Background Unit

This standard notation drum pattern demonstrates an eighth note background unit.

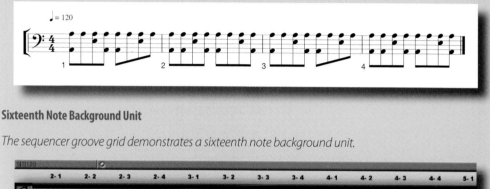

Sixteenth Note Background Unit

The sequencer groove grid demonstrates a sixteenth note background unit.

Kick and Snare Pattern

Once the background unit is defined, the kick and snare patterns work together to define the feeling and momentum of the groove. A constant hi-hat along with the kick and snare are the essence of a live groove as played by a drummer.

The snare drum is typically played primarily on beats two and four. Often the snare is also played on the eighth note after two and/or four, or on the sixteenth note before beat one and/or three.

Ghost Notes

The snare drum often plays ghost notes on some or all of the background unit notes. These ghost notes are played very softly and aren't meant to be heard—they're meant to be felt. Ghost notes help the drummer lock into the groove, playing steady time with a musical feel.

In creating a realistic groove, ghost notes help the rhythm feel like a human played it rather than a computer. Keep the ghost notes at very low levels—they must be felt and not heard. Often these ghost notes are played by the left hand in opposition to the constant pattern played by the right hand. For example, if the right hand is playing straight eighth notes, the left hand will often play the second, fourth, sixth, eighth, twelfth, fourteenth, and sixteenth notes quietly on the snare drum between the primary snare beats.

Video Example 6-1

Ghost Notes on the Snare Drum during a Live Drum Groove

Quantizing the Groove

Quantizing is a standard MIDI process in which the performance of the beats into the sequencer is adjusted to conform to the user-selected background unit. The computer moves every note of the pattern to the closest background unit. When you select a range of MIDI notes and select Quantize from your sequencer menu, the computer moves every note of the pattern to the closest background unit.

The up side of the quantizing process is that it instantly tightens the groove, making it perfectly accurate. The down side of the quantizing process is that it removes any human tendency from the groove. Any natural and authentic feel that the performer provided when the groove was recorded is cleaned up.

On the surface, it might seem like a good idea to make the groove mathematically perfect. In reality, the feel—the result of human excitement or compassion—is transmitted through human beat-placement tendencies. A human performance, along with its very imperfect beat placement, compels the listener to join in with the song's energy—a mathematically perfect groove feels very stiff and rigid.

For most productions, try to keep at least some of the tendencies of the human performance. This will help provide grooves that are useful in productions and powerful in feel. Most modern DAWs provide access to several quantizing parameters. If you quantize with the sensitivity set to less than 100 percent, the computer will only draw the performance that percentage of the way to the mathematically perfect position. Set the sensitivity between 40 and 90 percent to retain some of the human feel in your groove while still tightening the feel.

It is by no means mandatory that you quantize the groove patterns. However, if you want to maintain the human feel of the MIDI perfor-mance, be sure that your sequencing software is set to the maximum resolution. Early sequencers divided a quarter note into 48 or 96 units (ticks.) Any real-time performance was forced to fit these units; however, this resolution is not fine enough to record real-time input. Performances that were not quantized typically felt very awkward and cumbersome on these early sequencers.

Modern sequencers have very fine resolution, with the quarter note typically divided into at least 960 ticks. These sequencers provide adequate resolution to accurately record a real-time performance.

The other primary consideration whenever you are recording real-time into a sequencer is the proficiency of the performer. If the performer is incapable of an excellent performance, you'll usually need to provide some quantizing help. On the other hand, if the musician plays with great virtuosity, take advantage of the energy and passion conveyed through an excellent performance by recording the track in real time.

There will be more information about quantizing options in the upcoming chapters on MIDI recording and production.

Pushing, Relaxed, or on Top of the Beat

If you're a passionate listener of music, you've probably noticed that some drummers and grooves feel very aggressive—they tend to make you lean forward in anticipation of what will happen next. On the other hand, you've probably noticed that other grooves are calming—they're very laid back and they tend to make you feel relaxed. Still other grooves feel tight, precise, and sometimes mechanical—they're typically right on the beat.

Real human drummers all have beat-placement tendencies that are derived largely from their personality. A drummer that is more aggressive—some might say hyper—probably plays a groove a little ahead of the beat. A drummer who is mellow and relaxed is likely to play behind the beat. Even though drums are often performed in reference to a constant click track, the drummer's natural rhythmic tendencies will probably show through.

If you want to create a groove that feels edgy and aggressive, try shifting the snare, the hi-hat, or even the entire drum track slightly ahead of the beat. This could provide the emotional change that helps the song come alive. If you want the groove to feel laid back, try moving the kick and snare later by a few ticks.

Moving beats around like this, by shifting notes and tracks, is a very common procedure in the pursuit of the perfect groove. Small changes in placement affect the feeling of the entire production.

Audio Example 6-1

Varying the Groove Feel

Each genre has fundamental tendencies in the stylistically appro-priate rhythmic feel. As you develop productions for different styles of music, make it your goal to become familiar with the characteristics and tendencies of the specific genre. When you're producing hip-hop, reggae, zydeco, speed metal, and so on, you need to know the rhythmic, harmonic, and idiomatically characteristic aspects of great productions. Immerse yourself in the specifics of the genre you're producing—listen to albums, read books, or do whatever it takes. iTunes and other Internet music providers are excellent resources for gaining great insight into a musical style without spending hundreds of dollars.

Basic Percussion

Once you've defined the feel and structure, the loop is nearly completed. Often simple grooves work best in a musical setting.

Most basic drum set grooves sound even more powerful when combined with a few simple percussion instruments. Add a shaker playing along with the background unit or a tambourine on beats two and four.

The shaker rhythm often highlights a set of accents that help add momentum and energy to the groove. Sometimes the tambourine accents beats two and four, while at the same time playing straight eighth or sixteenth notes. High and low conga drums support the snare on beat two along with beat four and the "and" of four. Standard triangle, guiro, cabasa, cowbell, and clave patterns almost always augment the basic drum groove.

Non-traditional synth effects and sampled sounds often fill out the groove texture in a way that adds color and emotion to a loop. The only disadvantage to incorporating sounds that are outside the normal list of groove instruments is that they quickly catch the listener's attention and tend to lose their effectiveness rapidly. Most sounds that are outside the norm should be used primarily for occasional contrast.

Audio Example 6-2

Non-Traditional Sounds in the Groove

Sampled Sounds and Custom Samples

Custom loops don't have to consist exclusively of custom samples and sounds. They are custom in that they're composed for a specific purpose and are uniquely part of a personal custom library. On the other hand, including your own custom samples along with stock sounds helps define a unique character and personality.

Loops are obviously not limited to drums and percussion; however, these fundamental ingredients provide the foundation for many projects. Once the rhythmic foundation is established, bass, guitar, synth, and other instrumental and vocal loops augment the production nicely. Most of the time, though, musicians perform along with the foundational loops to provide ingredients that are specifically inspired by the song and production needs.

When loops are used in sweetening rather than in basic tracking, they're typically very simple and thematic melodic ideas, introduced a few times during the production. These simple loops provide a catchy musical "hook" that helps draw the listener into the musical sound-scape.

Saving Multiple Versions

Once you have built up a large and impressive pattern that creates the feel and emotion inspired by your musical needs, record a stereo audio track of the entire groove. This is the source for the pattern that will be looped.

Record the loop into the same DAW that it was constructed on so the stereo track is embedded with the proper tempo information. This way, the loop can eventually follow the tempo change of the sequence in which it is used.

Record several versions of the same loop. Once the full version is completed satisfactorily, record simplified and streamlined versions of the loop. In addition to the basic groove and variations, record versions that contain fills, such as the type you would expect to lead into a new musical section. It's usually sufficient to include three to six fill variations. If you want your productions to sound professional, avoid using the same fill pattern multiple times throughout a production.

A typical list of loops generated from a DAW might look like the following:

- Full version (Kick pattern 1)
- Full version (Kick pattern 2)
- Fill pattern 1
- Fill pattern 2
- Fill pattern 3
- No percussion
- Percussion only
- Drum kit and tambourine
- Tambourine only
- Tambourine and shaker

Variations of the Groove

The illustration below demonstrates the variations in a couple commercial loop libraries. Based on their experience, these companies have decided that it takes several versions of each groove to build an authentic and natural song.

The list below from Spectrasonics' Stylus RMX contains drum and percussion loops that work very well alone or when layered together.

STYLUS RMX — SPECTRASONICS

Elements [SETTINGS]

```
098-Peppers 1
098-Peppers 2
098-Peppers 3
098-Peppers 4
098-Peppers FBar 1
098-Peppers FBar 2
098-Peppers FBar 3
098-Peppers FBar 4
098-Peppers Fill a
098-Peppers Fill b
098-Peppers Fill c
098-Peppers Fill d
```

bigfishaudio.com

```
02 112 D .aif
02 112 D bass.aif
02 112 D clavinet 01.aif
02 112 D clavinet 02.aif
02 112 D congas 01.aif
02 112 D congas 02.aif
02 112 D congas 03.aif
02 112 D drums 01.aif
02 112 D drums 02.aif
02 112 D drums 03.aif
02 112 D drums fill.aif
02 112 D guitar.aif
02 112 D horns.aif
02 112 D scratch fx.aif
02 112 D synth 01.aif
02 112 D synth 02.aif
```

The list above is from Big Fish Audio's Funk City library. It contains several drum and percussion loops along with bass, guitar, synth, and horn loops. They all work together in a very musical way.

Building a Loop from Complete Recordings

Many loops are created from existing recordings. As long as you get complete legal permission and have met all conditions, sampling grooves and riffs from previously recorded music is an exciting way to capture a specific musical feel. Building your musical production around an established groove foundation produces very quick results.

A typical production based on a previously recorded loop defines the foundation of the recording, alternating between a drum groove (possibly with bass guitar) and one or two loops with the same groove accompanied by a simple instrumental lick. Creativity operates in the organization and augmentation of a few fundamental ingredients.

Set the Loop Tempo

When you are creating loops of drum and percussion grooves that you have recorded as performed by live musicians, it's most convenient to record directly into your digital recording software or DAW in reference to a click track. Be sure that the recording is directly linked to the sequence click tempo. This timing information will stay with the loop once it is edited and defined.

Fit the Loop to the Sequence Tempo

The most basic consideration when sampling and looping existing music is that it loops seamlessly. The pattern, riff, or groove must play constantly with absolutely no hint of awkwardness in timing or texture. This might require a fair amount of trimming of length along with crossfading between the end and beginning of the loop.

Whenever importing audio into a DAW for looping, match the sequence tempo as closely as possible to the audio tempo. When the editing process is complete you will need to adjust the loop to fit precisely within the number of beats and measures you've chosen for the loop length.

Start and End the Loop at Zero Amplitude

Once the audio is recorded or imported, locate the segment for looping and edit it so the loop starts exactly when beat one happens. In your recording software, it will usually be obvious where the first beat of the pattern is located. Trim off all excess audio right up to the point where the audio wave of beat one crosses the zero-amplitude axis in an upward direction. Zoom in closely to be certain that you're starting the audio at the zero point. If the loop starts at positive or negative amplitude, there is more likelihood that the loop will click or glitch as it repeats.

In the same manner, once you have located the end of the loop, zoom in to verify that the actual end of the loop is crossing the zero-amplitude axis from below. When the loop's start point is crossing the axis in an upward direction and the end point is crossing from below, there is reasonable assurance that the loop will repeat with no glitch or click.

Loop Start and End Points

Trim off the beginning and end of each loop so that it starts and ends at zero amplitude. Once the basic timing for the loop is established, simply trim to the closest zero amplitude in order to minimize the risk of pops or clacks as the loop repeats each time, or as a series of loops are chained together.

The multitrack loop below illustrates a multitrack loop that starts and ends at zero amplitude.

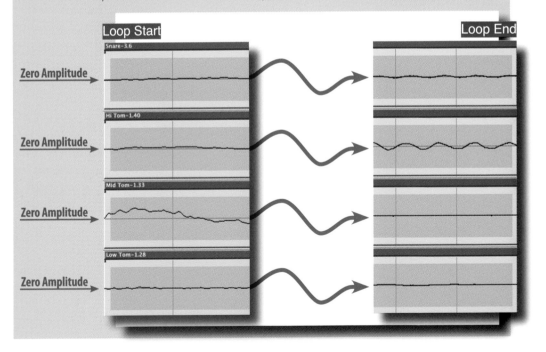

Conform the Loop to the Sequence Beat Grid

Once the loop length is established, either conform the loop to the sequencer beat grid or conform the beat grid to the loop. It's important that the loop is functional within any software or hardware DAW. If you have closely set the sequence tempo to the loop tempo, the simplest way to make sure the loop tempo tag is accurate is to use the time compression and expansion features of the recording software to physically fit the loop into the measure range that matches the loop.

The advantage of this process is that it is very fast, although the purist would prefer to maintain the original sample specifications without time adjustments, which require interpolation and conversion of the original data. Realistically, most loops require some time adjustment within a production anyway, whether manually or automatically, in order to match the sequence tempo. When the loop fits the measure range perfectly, be sure to set the loop tempo to match the sequence tempo.

The other option to match the loop tempo with the sequence is to adjust the sequence tempo in small increments until the measure range of the sequence perfectly matches the loop length. This routine requires much more tedious experimentation than time-altering the loop to fit the sequence; however, modern digital recording applications provide fractional tempo adjustments, typically in hundredths of a beat per minute. Adjusting the tempo so that the loop fits perfectly into the loop's measure range maintains the original data in its pure, unaltered form. Once the tempo has been established, be sure to save the loop referenced to the precise sequence tempo.

Placing the Loop in a Sequence

Once you begin to use your custom loops in productions, you'll quickly realize the wisdom in the recommendations in this chapter so far. The tempo information that resides with the stored audio loop is used to automatically adjust the loop to the tempo of your production.

Loop management and playback software recognize the tempo information in the loop. As each loop is imported into a production, it is automatically adjusted to fit the tempo beat grid. This convenience ensures effortless production of high-quality music using loops that show up ready to rock.

Digital recording software provides tempo data recognition in each imported audio sound bite. Typically, the loop is imported in reference to its original tempo tag; however, modern recording software and DAWs provide options to adjust the loop to the sequence tempo or the sequence tempo to the loop tempo.

If the loop has been edited properly and the tempo has been set accurately, the import and tempo adjustment process is very easy. Sometimes the loop doesn't fit exactly into the beat grid like it should. In this case, you still need to adjust the loop length so it fits perfectly into the loop's original measure range.

When the loop is placed into your recording software, always loop the audio within an even measure range. Simply looping the audio in whatever length it imports will typically create timing discrepancies later in the sequence.

Video Example 6-3

Placing the Loop and Adjusting the Tempo

Label Loops with Tempo Information

As you build your loop library, label each loop in a group with the same basic name, augmenting each to indicate the type of variation it represents. Additionally, include a tempo reference in the name. The tempo reference helps you know the original tempo before you place the loop in a sequence. The farther the original tempo is from the new sequence tempo, the more dramatic the conversion and interpolation process and therefore the more potentially damaging the process is to the loop audio quality.

A label such as "Funk_Grv001_Full01_125" indicates the family ("Funk_Grv001"), the variation ("Full01"), and the original tempo ("125"). All of this information is very useful and it sorts well in an alphabetical list.

The Feel

The primary reasons that loops became so popular so quickly were their authentic rhythmic feel and their ease of use. In an era when most home recordists were struggling to create their own drum and percussion tracks, loops instantly boosted their production quality. Professionals using professional-level equipment recorded the loops, and highly skilled musicians typically performed them. The rhythmic feel provided by the loops was on one hand nearly perfect and on the other hand authentic and human.

As you create loops of all kinds, maintain very high standards in relation to the technical and musical quality. It's usually obvious to most musicians when a groove just feels good—everybody in the room recognizes it when it happens. Strive to record loop source material that feels great from a musical standpoint.

When the groove is recorded and placed on a beat grid, commonly included in audio recording software, it's a simple process to zoom in on the groove waveform to see how the recorded beats line up with the mathematically perfect beat grid. Resist the tendency to instantly start adjusting beats so they line up with the beat grid. Loop the groove and listen to it play back. If there is a beat that consistently feels odd, edit that beat so the groove flows well. If the loop feels great with no editing, consider your mission accomplished and save it in your loop library.

Using Loops Together

Not all loops work well together. Since human feel is a desired ingredient in loops, one loop might have a very laid back and relaxed feel, while another loop might have a very aggressive and hyper feel. Loops with dramatically different musical feels typically don't sound good together in the same production—they constantly fight each other, creating an uneasy musical feeling.

Layering loops of live performances requires a good understanding of musical feel and beat tendencies. As you're recording loop source material, intentionally develop libraries of aggressive and laid back loops. A good musician is in control of beat placement. If you ask a great drummer to lay the groove back, he or she will typically delay the kick and/or snare ever so slightly. Conversely, when instructed to make a groove feel more aggressive, the drummer will move specific groove ingredients slightly forward in the timeline. These beat placement changes are very subtle in most cases, but they create extremely different musical grooves.

Video Example 6-4

Layering Loops in Stylus RMX, Mach 5, and GarageBand

Drum Kit

In terms of the number of drums, it doesn't take a large drum kit to create a great loop—it's all about the feel. You need to get the sounds right, but you definitely need to get the perfect feel from the drummer.

A kit with a kick, snare, and hi-hat provides plenty of sound to create usable grooves. Variations in the patterns between these three ingredients provide excellent flow, and combining the different loop versions throughout the production is very representative of how a real drummer might react during a topnotch performance. Additionally, the simple setup provides a very close and intimate drum sound.

Miking the Drum Kit

Combine close and distant microphones to achieve the drum sound that fits your production. A typical multitrack setup uses condenser mics for overheads and hi-hats, along with moving coil mics for close-miking the individual drums. Once you're able to get a great drum sound using the traditional setup, experiment with non-traditional techniques to create a unique, characteristic sound.

Typical drum mic setup

1. Kick - inside
2. Kick - outside
3. Snare
4. Tom
5. Tom
6. Tom
7. Tom
8. Overhead left
9. Overhead right
10. Hi-hat

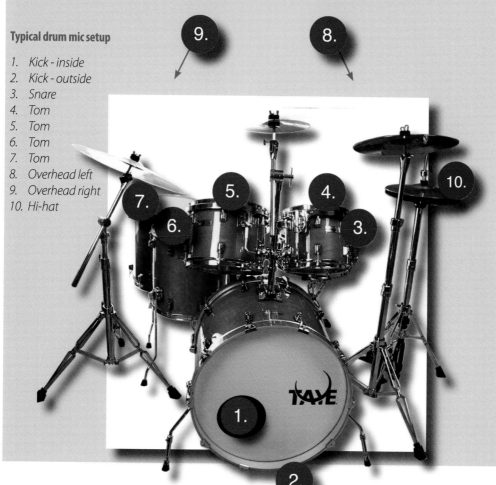

As the size of the drum kit expands to include several cymbals and toms, the intimacy of the recorded sound is often adversely affected. When you record drums for loop source material, set up a mix of the drum tracks that includes only the tracks that are active. If the toms are not playing, turn the tom tracks down or off; if the ride cymbal isn't playing, turn the ride cymbal mic down or off; and so on. This procedure helps produce the most powerful drum loops. Extraneous room ambience creates a distant and amateurish sound. Control the mix and only include what you really want to include.

If you are recording loops in a professional studio or any room that enhances the drum sound, the most blended and musical sound might include ambience and leakage into open mics. Adjust the mix according to your musical needs. Sometimes, a drum sound that is too tight and controlled doesn't blend well with the rest of the instruments.

Mike the kit in the same way you would during a tracking session and always consider the impact and feel that works for your specific musical production. Refer to *The S.M.A.R.T. Guide to Recording Great Audio Tracks in a Small Studio* for fundamental drum-miking techniques.

Percussion Kit

Anything that can be hit falls into the percussion category. If you've ever hired or performed with a serious percussionist in the recording world, you probably know that his or her kit includes everything from cymbals to cereal boxes to brake drums. These unique and interesting sounds are truly magical when creatively included in almost any musical production.

Most percussionists are aware of the microphones around them. When recording a percussion kit to a multitrack recorder, set up a basic stereo-miking configuration, and then augment with a few close mics. Set the close mics on congas or bongos to keep them in close perspective in the mix. In addition, set a microphone or two specifically for auxiliary percussion instruments, such as triangles, keys, shakers, and so on. The percussionist should understand that the transient content of each instrument dictates that a distance of one or two feet from the mic is typically close enough to provide a sufficiently intimate sound.

If you want an accurate and transparent sound, use condenser mics for the percussion kit. Almost every percussion instrument produces

Contrasts in the Groove Texture

Plan your arrangement so that there is contrast in texture and growth in momentum. In the same way we contrast dynamics, we should also contrast orchestration textures. In fact, most recordings maintain a similar full level throughout the entire arrangement; contrasts might seem dynamic but they are more typically textural.

The illustration below simply demonstrates changes in orchestration through the addition and subtraction of mix ingredients.

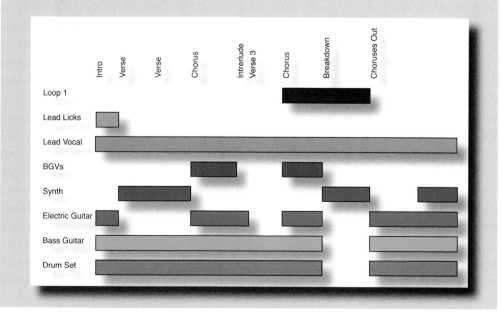

abundant transient information, so the accuracy and efficiency of the condenser mic capsule is best suited to accurate percussion recording.

Most percussion recordings are intended to accurately capture the natural sound of each instrument; however, these sounds are also very interesting when processed through a number of effects. When you're sampling and creating loops, experiment with various effects to create unique and interesting sounds.

Supporting the Drums with Percussion

The most convenient way to support a specific groove with percussion instruments is to actually perform the percussion tracks while monitoring the groove that has been looped. Have the percussionist perform along with the groove, and then select the patterns that best support the groove to separate out as a loop. As long as their length fits evenly with the groove loop, you'll be able to place the percussion tracks according to the musical considerations when developing your production. Because they're performed in reference to the groove, all percussion tracks should fit perfectly with the groove feel.

Build the percussion track so that it flows with the orchestration and production. The entrance of the perfect percussion part at a musical section change provides momentum and textural flow. Then, once the percussion part thins out, the equally dramatic contrast helps guide the listener's focus through the arrangement.

Video Example 6-5

Contrast in the Groove Texture

Guitar Riffs

Guitar riffs and comps that work well in the context of loops are often simple and catchy. Single-note comps with varying textures that are tonally vague work well throughout most chord progressions that consist of diatonic tonality. Licks consisting of the first, second, fifth, and sixth steps of the major scale tend to be tonally neutral.

Interesting chord comps are very useful. When the chord comp defines specific tonality within the key, be sure to record multiple compatible comps that offer options as the chord progression unfolds though the song.

To record excellent source material for your loops, have the guitarist play along with interesting chord progressions, and then edit the comps after the fact into separate loops that can be combined no matter where the chord progression goes.

If you would like a model of excellent guitar samples, check out the "Raging Guitars" library from Big Fish Audio. The sounds are great and the samples are intelligently laid out.

Video Example 6-6

Guitar Comps, Licks, and Riffs

Bass Loops

Bass grooves are very powerful, especially in a genre that has minimal tonality changes. Record a musically excellent bassist performing bass patterns that follow a basic chord progression, or record idiomatically impressive bass licks that will work together in your loop-based sequence to create an awesome bass track.

Record the bassist performing with several standard chord progressions in several styles and tempos, and then edit the recording into several loops that can be combined in any order that matches the chord progression of your production.

Many home recordists can play basic bass guitar parts but lack the virtuosity to perform very technically demanding snaps and thumps that are predominant in some genres. If you want to develop a library of bass loops that will allow you to create bass parts far above your bass virtuosity, record several different idiomatic bass effects. Record several thumb and finger slaps, hammer-ons, pull-offs, snaps, and plucks. Use these ingredients to structure interesting musical parts. Once the part is created, record the part onto a track as a continuous audio segment that can be edited into a loop.

Video Example 6-7

Bass Groove Sounds and Segments

Keyboard Loops

Keyboard loops, like guitar loops, are often very simple and generic. The array of possible keyboard sounds is immense. Therefore, most keyboard sounds and musical parts are constructed and designed specifically for each production.

Loops that are generated from keyboards and synthesizers are often sound-effects-oriented rather than pitch-oriented. Spend some time to build interesting sound effects and processed percussion-like sounds. Then sample them and construct rhythmic patterns that will eventually be saved and edited into loops that can be used to augment your productions. It's often very convenient to have these loops available to support the produced groove. Also, it is typically the best approach to save these sound effects as independent samples that can be structured specifically for your musical needs.

Long Loops

Although most loops are one, two, or four measures long, there are also many reasons to create longer loops. First, it is always easy to edit one-, two-, and four-bar loops out of a great eight- or 16-bar loop. Second, loops that are eight or 16 measures long provide an excellent resource in song development. Because the majority of songs utilize sections that are eight bars long, recording variations of the same groove that are eight measures long is very useful. In regard to drum-kit loops, the intro is often open, with the drummer playing the ride cymbal as the background unit. The verse often comes down to a simpler groove with the hi-hat providing the background unit. The chorus typically comes back up in intensity, and the bridge either steps up the intensity again or strips the groove down to a minimal level. On a solo section, the drum groove often stays about the same as the bridge with a slight variation in the kick or snare pattern.

If you record multiple eight-bar loops with these types of textural changes in mind, your loops will be very usable on many productions. To get the most out of the live drum tracks that you record specifically for one song, go back after the fact and edit the intro, verse, chorus, bridge, and solo section into separate loops that can be applied to future productions.

As you build long loops, take advantage of the increased flexibility of saving them as multitrack loops that can be edited and remixed in response to the needs of each specific production.

Saving in the Appropriate Formats

Whenever you're developing loops, save them in the highest-resolution format possible. There's no reason to save the loops at a greater resolution than they were recorded at. If the loops were recorded at 44.1 kHz/16 bit, save them at that resolution because there's no real benefit from converting up, other than to match the resolution of a future production. However, if the loop is recorded at 192 kHz/24 bit, be sure to save it at that resolution.

When you use the loops in a production and you need to convert the sample or bit rates, be certain that you keep the loop in its original format using a converted clone for your production. Conversion tends to diminish digital audio quality, so maintain access to your original unconverted loops.

As you build a project, save the loops you use into a separate folder that resides in your project folder. If you always save the loops with your project, there will be few problems reconstructing the production for future remixes or further production.

The professional audio formats are primarily AIFF and WAV files. Record and save your files in the highest possible resolution AIFF or WAV formats. There is no reason to save files in compressed or down-converted forms because the audio data can easily be adjusted for future productions. In addition, future conversion algorithms and processes might be far superior to existing methods.

MIDI Basic Training

This chapter covers the fundamentals of the MIDI process. I won't cover every parameter here, but I will cover the features and parameters you must understand to address and successfully operate most of the newer MIDI-based devices. Hardware-based sequencers, software-based sequencers, digital audio workstations, drum sequencers, signal processors, mixers, and notation software packages all use MIDI as a central control and communication language. Most of the information in this chapter applies to the practical use of these key tools in the audio, video, and multimedia industries.

Although MIDI is somewhat old news for a third-millennium book, it still pertains directly to the operation of many current and forthcoming mixers and processors. Not only do many digital audio software packages use MIDI parameters to control mixdown, but many hardware mixers use MIDI to automate and control all audio parameters—sequenced and digitally recorded.

With an understanding of the information in this chapter, you should be able to easily and willingly tackle any MIDI equipment you'll encounter. There are no mysteries to MIDI. The system is logical and powerful.

Introduction to MIDI

The first MIDI sequencer I had was a Yamaha TX-7. It did next to nothing compared to the tools we have available today, and it did it in such a cumbersome way that it was hard to get motivated to use it. Then I was introduced to my first Macintosh 512 with rev. 1.0 of Performer, the hottest sequencing package from Mark of the Unicorn. Now we were talking! MIDI sequencing that was easy to use, made sense, and was designed to be used by musicians. Heaven! Sequencing packages today are amazing, and the manufacturers are very competitive. Even if one company develops an edge, the rest follow quickly behind with nearly identical features. Fine sequencing software is also available from Opcode, Digidesign, and many others. These sequencing tools have revolutionized the way we can all work. We've worked through the initial obsession of trying to produce complete MIDI projects, and we can now go ahead and combine real instruments and musicians with MIDI instruments and digital audio. And it's only going to get better. I really think the twenty-first century will see amazing applications for holography, virtual reality, and multisensory recording and playback. Wherever our minds can wander, technology will follow.

The Language

MIDI has been the fundamental Musical Instrument Digital Interface since the early '80s. It behooves us to understand the communication principles involved in MIDI data transfer, even as newer and more improved formats evolve.

MIDI is nothing more than a common language used by synthesizers, sound modules, and any other MIDI-implemented instruments to communicate either with each other or with a hardware- or software-based MIDI sequencer. A MIDI interface is simply an interpreter to assist in communications between the MIDI instrument and a computer.

The communication language is based on a hexadecimal (16-digit) binary code. In other words, each parameter and function of a MIDI device is represented by a unique arrangement of 16 ones and zeros.

MIDI Communication

Anytime a note is played or a controller is used, its unique binary code is transmitted from the MIDI Out port. The code is then received by another synth through the MIDI in port. When the synth recognizes the unique binary code for whatever MIDI parameter has been transmitted, it, too, responds to the command. This process takes about three milliseconds.

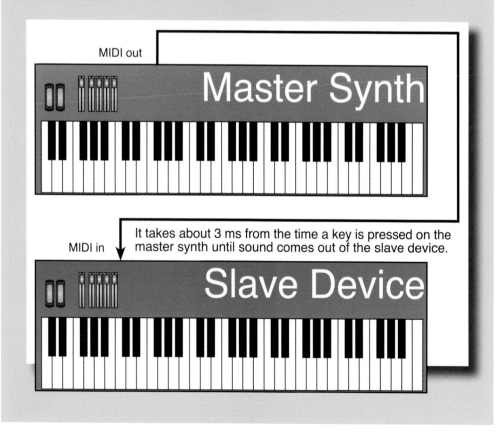

MIDI out

Master Synth

It takes about 3 ms from the time a key is pressed on the master synth until sound comes out of the slave device.

MIDI in

Slave Device

Middle C on the synthesizer keyboard is assigned a unique and specific binary number. Any time that note is played, its unique binary code is transmitted from the MIDI Out port. That code is then received by another synth through the MIDI In port. When the synth recognizes the unique binary code for middle C it, too, plays middle C. This process takes about three milliseconds.

This simple concept is applied to each MIDI parameter, forming a powerful and musically efficient means of communication in the electronic music genre. The list of MIDI-controllable parameters is extensive, ranging from note value to portamento value to poly/mono/omni mode selection.

MIDI In, Out, and Thru

There are typically three MIDI ports on the back of a MIDI device: MIDI In, MIDI Out, and MIDI Thru.

To connect MIDI equipment together, connect the MIDI Out of the controlling device to the MIDI In of the device being controlled.

MIDI Ports

There are typically three MIDI ports on the back of a MIDI device: MIDI in, MIDI out, and MIDI thru. A 5-pin DIN connector and jack are used to interconnect MIDI devices.

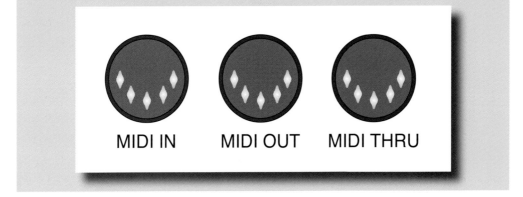

MIDI IN   MIDI OUT   MIDI THRU

Once you have successfully completed this connection, the pathway is clear for communication.

MIDI Connection

To connect MIDI equipment together, connect the MIDI out of the controlling device (Master) to the MIDI in of the device being controlled (Slave). Once this connection has been successfully completed, the pathway is clear for communication. Remember, MIDI cables carry controlling data only. They don't carry audio signals.

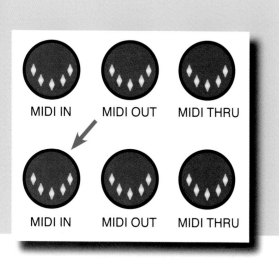

MIDI Cables

MIDI cables use a standard 5-pin DIN connector. The cable is similar to a mic cable in that it utilizes a twisted pair of conductors surrounded by a shield. Even though the connector has five pins, only three are in use for the standard MIDI format. Pins 1 and 3 (the outer two pins) are not connected in the classic MIDI cable—they're left for future development and manufacturer-specific design. Pin 2 is connected to the shield for ground, and pins 4 and 5 are used to conduct the MIDI data.

It's even possible to make adapter cables with the 5-pin DIN connector on one end and a standard XLR connector on the other. Because both standards only use three pins, there's no loss when converting to XLR. Simply connect pin 2 of the DIN connector to pin 1 of the XLR, and then connect DIN pins 4 and 5 to XLR pins 2 and 3.

Adapters like this can enable a MIDI signal to pass through an already existing microphone patch panel—a very handy feature when trying to run the sound module (in the control room) from the keyboard (in the studio). Avoid any MIDI cable run longer than 50 feet.

MIDI Pin Numbers

Pins 1 and 3 (the outer two pins) are not connected in the classic MIDI cable—they're left for future development and manufacturer-specific design. Pin 2 is connected to the shield for ground, and pins 4 and 5 are used to transmit the MIDI data.

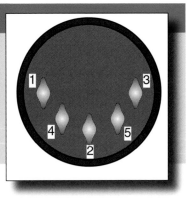

Daisy Chain

If you'd like to control two separate MIDI devices with one controller, connect the MIDI Out of the controlling device to MIDI In of the first device being controlled, and then connect the MIDI Thru of that device to MIDI In of the second device being controlled. This procedure is called daisy chaining. It isn't the best way to connect several MIDI devices together, but it is an acceptable setup if you don't connect more than a few MIDI devices to the chain.

Remember, each additional device adds approximately a three-millisecond delay to the chain. So, if you use three keyboards (one controller and two sound modules), the first module would be delayed three milliseconds and the second would be delayed six milliseconds. If you keep the instruments that need to rhythmically lock together (such as drums and bass) at the very front of the daisy chain and instruments with slower attacks (such as strings) at the rear of the chain, all should be well.

If you're using a computer-based sequencer, chances are the sequencer program will let you shift tracks in time. Try shifting each track in the daisy chain forward in multiples of three milliseconds, depending on which link each part is in the chain.

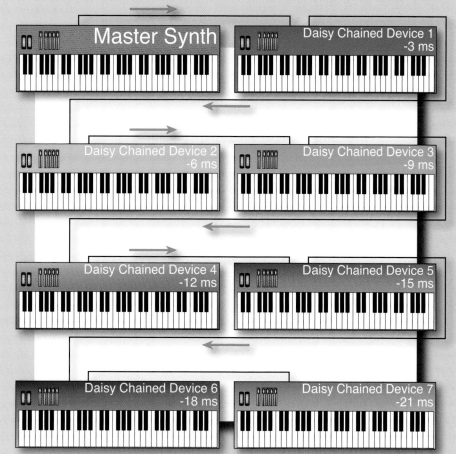

Daisy Chaining

Remember, each additional device in the chain adds another three milliseconds to the MIDI delay. Therefore, if you use three keyboards (one controller and two sound modules), the first module would be delayed three milliseconds and the second would be delayed six milliseconds. Keep the instruments that need to rhythmically lock together, such as drums and bass, at the very front of the daisy chain. Keep instruments with slower attacks (like strings) at the rear of the chain.

Master Synth

Daisy Chained Device 1
-3 ms

Daisy Chained Device 2
-6 ms

Daisy Chained Device 3
-9 ms

Daisy Chained Device 4
-12 ms

Daisy Chained Device 5
-15 ms

Daisy Chained Device 6
-18 ms

Daisy Chained Device 7
-21 ms

Listen to Audio Example 7-1 to hear the effect of daisy chaining. By the time the seventh slave device has received its MIDI data there's a noticeable delay. Using these percussive sounds, it's clear that there's an adverse rhythmic consequence when daisy chaining.

Audio Example 7-1

Daisy Chain Delay

Channels

The MIDI communication language provides an option that is not only convenient, but also essential when you are using multiple MIDI sound sources. MIDI channels help the sound modules or synths determine which data to receive. You can send the piano, bass, drums, and so on all at once, in the same MIDI data stream. If you select MIDI channel 1 for the piano send, channel 2 for the bass, and channel 3 for the drums, you can send them, even through a daisy chain, to three separate sound modules. Simply set the piano module to receive only MIDI channel 1, the bass module to receive only MIDI channel 2, and the drum module to receive only channel 3. The modules will sift through all the MIDI data and receive only that which is tagged as belonging to its channel.

There are 16 standard MIDI channels written into the MIDI language specification; therefore, in theory, you could daisy chain up to 16 sound modules, instructing each module to receive a unique MIDI channel. In other words, you could send 16 separate musical parts—one to each module. This approach is often unacceptable because by the time the signal reaches the end of the daisy chain, the signal has been delayed by about 45 milliseconds. That's a substantial delay.

The multicable MIDI interface is the answer to this delay problem.

MIDI Interface

Even though MIDI is a computer language, it doesn't naturally fit into the operating system of most computers. A MIDI interface is the actual hardware that transforms the MIDI language into a format that can be sent and received from a computer. Most workstations contain their own internal MIDI interface that interprets data for the built-in processor. Some computers are equipped with an internal MIDI interface, but typically the most flexible and expandable approach involves an external interface.

Some interfaces are very simple, containing one or two MIDI inputs and one or two MIDI outputs. For a small system that uses only a few synths or sound modules, this type of interface works very well.

With the advent of multichannel sound modules and MIDI-controlled mixers and processors, the MIDI language by itself runs out of gas quickly. It's simply not practical to daisy chain everything together, and many MIDI instruments can send and receive 16 MIDI channels at once.

Instruments capable of receiving more than one MIDI channel at the same time are called *multitimbral*. A common setup includes several multitimbral sound modules along with MIDI-controlled effects processors, a MIDI-controlled mixer, and probably MIDI machine control running the multitrack.

The multicable MIDI interface addresses this problem very sufficiently. Its basic operating principle is the same as the simple interface, although it processes all 16 MIDI channels though multiple cables. Most interfaces of this type offer eight separate cables that contain information for all 16 MIDI channels. This increases the power of MIDI dramatically. Not only does it multiply the available channels by the number of separate cables, but it sends all the data in perfect sync.

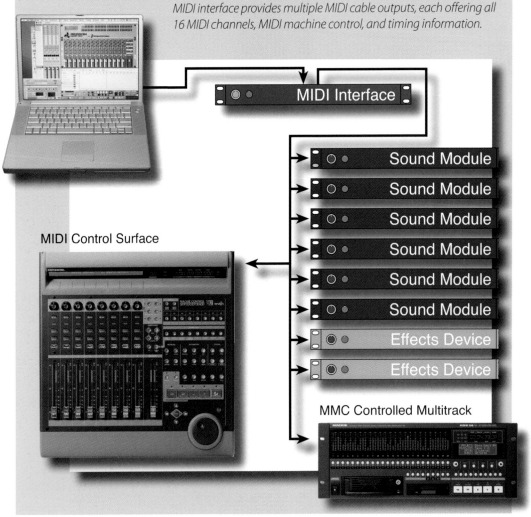

MIDI Controlled System

A common setup includes several multitimbral sound modules along with MIDI controlled effects processors, a MIDI control surface, and MIDI machine control running the multitrack. The most efficient MIDI interface provides multiple MIDI cable outputs, each offering all 16 MIDI channels, MIDI machine control, and timing information.

MIDI Interface

Sound Module

Sound Module

Sound Module

Sound Module

Sound Module

Sound Module

MIDI Control Surface

Effects Device

Effects Device

MMC Controlled Multitrack

Daisy chaining and its time delay problems become non-issues. You could use eight multitimbral sound modules with this type of interface and gain access to 128 MIDI channels! (That's eight cables multiplied by 16 MIDI channels.)

To add to the power offered by this kind of setup, the interfaces can usually be chained together. Four of these interfaces together would let you access 512 MIDI channels, although one would have to create quite a huge MIDI setup to need 512 MIDI channels.

Multicable MIDI Interface

The multicable MIDI interface sends all 16 MIDI channels simultaneously out of eight MIDI ports. Using this type of interface, the user can access up to eight multitimbral devices with absolutely no timing discrepancies among them. Devices can still be daisy chained from any of the MIDI outputs, but that's not typically necessary.

To add to the power offered by this kind of setup, the interfaces can usually be chained together. Four of these interfaces together would let you access 512 MIDI channels with no timing problems!

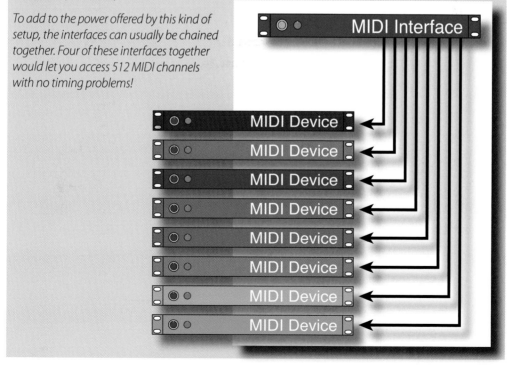

MIDI Parameters

The MIDI language has been developed to control almost any part of the performance imaginable. When a key is struck, a MIDI interpretation is rendered for the note name, as well as when it was struck; how fast it was struck; when it was released; what happened with the key pressure while it was sustained; whether and how a pedal, mod wheel, or pitch control was used; and the volume, pan, effects, and balance settings. There's also protocol for customizing the language for updates as well as instrument-specific instructions and commands.

The MIDI language only offers 128 steps of resolution (0–127). Therefore, if you use MIDI volume controller number 7 for a volume fade out, you don't really get an infinitely smooth fade, as you would with an analog fader. What you do get is a stair-step transition through 128 MIDI values. It's not likely that you'll hear each individual step, but sometimes the MIDI parameter adjustment is audible. We refer to this audible stair-step as the zipper effect.

Controllers

Many of the MIDI parameters deal with musical expression as it would be conveyed during a live performance. MIDI instruments use continuous and switched controllers to control things such as pitch bend, modulation, volume, and sustain. There are a total of 128 controllable parameters in MIDI spec. Controllers 0–63 are used as continuous controllers. Controllers 64–95 are used as switches. Controllers 96–121 are undefined, and 122–127 are reserved for channel mode messages.

Two or more performance wheels located to the left of the master keyboard typically vary these controller values. The performance wheels can usually be assigned to control any of the continuous controllers as well as some of the switched parameters. Aside from the performance

MIDI Controllers

There are a total of 128 controllable parameters in MIDI spec. Controllers 0–63 are used as continuous controllers. Controllers 64–95 are used as switches. Controllers 96–121 are undefined, and 122–127 are reserved for channel mode messages.

0	Bank Select	65	Portamento	92	Tremolo Depth (Effect 2)
1	Modulation Wheel	66	Sostenuto	93	Chorus Depth (Effect 3)
2	Breath Controller	67	Soft Pedal	94	Celeste Depth (Effect 4)
3	Undefined	68	Legato Footswitch	95	Phaser Depth (Effect 5)
4	Foot Controller	69	Hold 2	96	Data Increment
5	Portamento Time	70	Sound Variation/Exciter	97	Data Decrement
6	Data Entry	71	Harmonic	98	Nonregistered Parameter
7	Main Volume		Content/Compressor		Number LSB
8	Balance	72	Release Time/Distortion	99	Nonregistered Parameter
9	Undefined	73	Attack Time/Equalizer		Number MSB
10	Pan	74	Brightness/Expander-	100	Registered Parameter
11	Expression		Gate		Number LSB
12	Effect Control 1	75	Undefined/Reverb	101	Registered Parameter
13	Effect Control 2	76	Undefined/Delay		Number MSB
14	Undefined	77	Undefined/Pitch	102 – 119	
15	Undefined		Transpose		Undefined
16 –19		78	Undefined/Flange-Chorus	120	All Sound Off
	General Purpose 1 – 4	79	Undefined/Special Effects	121	Reset All Controllers
20 – 31		80 – 83		122	Local Control
	Undefined		General Purpose 5 – 8	123	All Notes Off
32 – 63		84	Portamento Control	124	Omni Mode Off
	LSB Value for	85 – 90		125	Omni Mode On
	Controllers 0 – 31		Undefined	126	Mono Mode On
64	Damper/Sustain Pedal	91	Effects Depth (Effect 1)	127	Poly Mode On

wheels, foot pedals can also access the controllable parameters, which are assignable to various MIDI control functions.

Channel Modes

Once communication is established between MIDI devices, the actual communication style must be selected. You must determine whether your MIDI devices should communicate to all channels, single channels, or any specified groups of channels by selecting the appropriate MIDI mode.

Omni Mode

A sound module set to omni MIDI mode hears and responds to all MIDI signals on all channels. This is not a common usage mode for song production, but it's a good mode for verifying connection between MIDI devices.

Multi Mode

Multi mode (multitimbral mode) is the most common MIDI working mode. Sound modules and synths set to multi mode discriminate between channel-specific signals. MIDI channel 1 only responds to information sent on channel 1, MIDI channel 2 only responds to information sent on channel 2, and so forth. This mode lets you develop the most individual parts from the available MIDI tools.

Mono Mode

Mono mode sets the synth to respond to only one note at a time. The original synths from Moog and Arp only had mono mode with no MIDI. They were simply single-voice oscillators with a set of filters to carve away at the sound. This subtractive form of synthesis had its own character and personality. To create a vintage musical line with a vintage synth feel, set up a fairly edgy sound in mono mode.

Mono mode is also applicable when you're driving a sound module with a guitar synthesizer, or any time you're trying to emulate an instrument that only emits one note at a time, such as a flute, clarinet, trumpet, or saxophone.

Polyphony versus Multitimbrality

Polyphony is simply the synth's ability to output more than one note at a time. Most modern synthesizers offer at least 32-voice polyphony; many offer 64-voice polyphony or more.

Whereas a polyphonic synth is capable of playing many notes at once, a multitimbral synth is capable of playing more than one MIDI channel at a time. Most modern synths and sound modules have

16-part multitimbrality—they can output sounds from all 16 MIDI channels at once.

Polyphonic voices are typically allocated to multitimbral MIDI channels on an as-needed basis. If your sound module has 32-voice polyphony, you could theoretically use seven voices on a piano harmony part, along with eight drum and percussion tracks, a six-voice string pad, a four-voice guitar part, a one-voice bass guitar track, a one-voice melody track, and a five-part brass section track before you ran out of voices—and that's only if all the parts were playing at once. Voice allocation uses whatever voices are available at any given moment. Your arrangement might only use 16 voices at the peak of its activity, so this type of arrangement would probably be pretty safe to perform on a 32-voice multitimbral sound module. Keep in mind, if any of the sounds you're using are layered, the number of voices used multiplies by the number of layers.

MIDI Time Code

MIDI Time Code is the MIDI equivalent to SMPTE Time Code. MIDI language converts the hours, minutes, seconds, frames, and subframes from SMPTE into MIDI commands. MIDI Time Code (MTC) lets MIDI devices communicate via a time-specific reference in much the same way a machine synchronizer communicates through SMPTE to match the time address of two mechanical drive systems.

System Exclusive Messages (Sys Ex)

Each manufacturer develops a communication language that's specific to its own gear. They customize their commands and develop product-specific languages for patch dumps, preset selections, editing parameters, and other special commands. All of these forms of data can be stored in a musical sequence, greatly increasing its power and flexibility. It also allows the accurate recall of sounds and adjustments that are so musically important; it's never fun to rebuild the sounds in a mix. System exclusive messages provide a means to restore the magic at a later date with minimal discomfort.

System exclusive data consists of three parts: the header, the body, and the "end of message" byte. The header simply identifies the manufacturer-specific codes; the body contains the actual data; and the end of message byte, F7, simply signifies the end of the sys ex transmission.

MIDI specification requires that system exclusive messages begin with F0 and end with F7. The body is determined by the equipment needs and the manufacturer's specifications. These messages vary in size but are always recorded as single events by a MIDI sequencer; therefore, on particularly large sys ex messages (some can be 10 to 20K), the sequencer might halt playback for a second or so while the data is transmitted. This can cause a problem if you don't strategically position sys ex data transmission within the sequence. It's typically workable to place sys ex transmissions at the beginning of the sequence, separated from the first MIDI note by a measure or so, depending on the amount of information that needs to be transferred. If the setup for a sequence requires a lot of system exclusive data, it's a good idea to place the sys ex data in a separate setup sequence.

A system exclusive message looks like a single line in most sequencing software packages. In reality, they are typically fairly large hexadecimal files. This data can usually be edited, but be sure to do your homework on the product before you start tweaking a system exclusive message—you could cause more problems than you solve.

System Exclusive Messages

In most software sequencers a system exclusive message looks like a single line of text on a long list. In reality, each line typically represents a fairly large hexadecimal file. System exclusive messages can usually be edited; however, be sure to do your homework on the product before tweaking a system exclusive message—you could cause more problems than you solve.

Each single system exclusive message actually contains several lines of code.

```
Length : 408      F0  F0        Ok   Cancel

  0:   F0 00 00 0E   0E 00 00 00   ........
  8:   60 2A 25 0B   67 28 0B 25   `*%.g‹.%
 10:   0B 1F 05 18   79 05 2A 41   ....y.*A
 18:   11 23 46 31   1B 06 40 1C   .#F1..@.
 20:   0E 73 36 6C   18 4C 30 6C   .s6l.L0l
 28:   18 40 2C 14   40 67 02 6C   .@,.@g.l
 30:   5B 04 52 17   41 06 00 10   [.R.A...
 38:   4B 29 46 37   60 02 10 4E   K)F7`..N
 40:   31 63 40 02   00 40 31 63   1c@..@1c
 48:   40 02 00 40   31 63 00 64   @..@1c.d
 50:   46 15 00 46   71 78 18 40   F..Fqx.@
 58:   31 4A 31 40   71 36 30 2C   1J1@q60,
 60:   61 0B 30 03   60 4B 47 01   a.0.`KG.
 68:   00 05 0A 0F   14 19 1E 23   .......#
 70:   28 2D 72 00   40 32 6C 00   (-r.@2l.
 78:   00 23 46 0C   63 36 0C 00   .#F.c6..
 80:   39 1C 66 6D   58 31 18 61   9.fmX1.a
 88:   58 31 00 59   28 00 4F 05   X1.Y(.O.
 90:   58 37 09 24   2F 02 00 00   X7.$/...
 98:   20 16 73 7A   1F 41 05 20   .sz.A.
 A0:   1C 63 46 01   05 00 00 63   .cF....c
 A8:   46 01 05 00   00 63 46 01   F.....cF.
 B0:   48 00 2B 00   0C 63 71 31   H.+..cq1
 B8:   00 63 14 63   00 63 6D 60   .c.c.cm`
 C0:   58 02 17 60   06 40 17 33   X..`.@.3
 C8:   01 00 0A 0A   1E 28 35 55   .....(5U
 D0:   4E 57 5A 64   01 20 60 15   NWZd. `.
 D8:   28 05 46 0C   19 46 6D 18   (.F..Fm.
 E0:   00 72 38 6C   5A 31 63 30   .r8lZ1c0
 E8:   42 31 63 34   7F 51 00 1E   B1c4.Q..
 F0:   0B 30 6F 12   48 5E 04 1A   .0o.H^..
 F8:   00 40 2C 26   19 56 01 0B   .@,&.V..
100:   40 38 46 0D   03 0A 00 00   @8F.....
108:   46 0D 03 0A   00 00 46 0D   F.....F.
110:   03 10 1B 56   00 18 46 63   ...V..Fc
118:   00 00 46 29   46 01 46 1B   c.F)F.F.
120:   40 31 05 2F   00 1C 00 2F   @1./.../
128:   0E 00 00 14   28 3C 50 64   ....(<Pd
130:   78 0C 21 35   49 03 00 41   x.!5l..A
138:   31 03 00 0C   19 32 0C 5B   1....2.[
140:   31 00 64 71   58 35 63 46   1.dqX5cF
148:   61 04 63 46   69 7E 23 01   a.cFi~#.
150:   3C 16 60 5E   25 10 3D 09   <.`%.=.
158:   34 00 00 59   4C 6B 4E 03   4  YLkO
```

```
▽ 📋 📑 📂 🎚 ① S  ⌁   Track-1 (Seq-
2|1|062 ⊡ ‹408› F0 00 00 0E 0E 00 00 00 60 2A 25
2|1|194 ⊡ ‹408› F0 00 00 0E 0E 00 00 01 00 64 02 2D
2|1|326 ⊡ ‹408› F0 00 00 0E 0E 00 02 00 42 1C 29
2|1|455 ⊡ ‹408› F0 00 00 0E 0E 00 03 00 60 12 03
2|2|105 ⊡ ‹408› F0 00 00 0E 0E 00 04 00 58 42 00
2|2|237 ⊡ ‹408› F0 00 00 0E 0E 00 05 00 5C 1E 01
2|2|367 ⊡ ‹408› F0 00 00 0E 0E 00 06 00 4C 02 29
2|3|016 ⊡ ‹408› F0 00 00 0E 0E 00 07 00 6E 10 13
2|3|151 ⊡ ‹408› F0 00 00 0E 0E 00 08 00 5A 02 25
2|3|280 ⊡ ‹408› F0 00 00 0E 0E 00 09 00 68 12 1D
2|3|410 ⊡ ‹408› F0 00 00 0E 0E 00 0A 00 46 18 03
2|4|062 ⊡ ‹408› F0 00 00 0E 0E 00 0B 00 48 12 0F
2|4|191 ⊡ ‹408› F0 00 00 0E 0E 00 0C 00 42 1C 03
2|4|326 ⊡ ‹408› F0 00 00 0E 0E 00 0D 00 68 1E 33
2|4|453 ⊡ ‹408› F0 00 00 0E 0E 00 0E 00 46 10 03
3|1|105 ⊡ ‹408› F0 00 00 0E 0E 00 0F 00 66 0A 05
3|1|237 ⊡ ‹408› F0 00 00 0E 0E 00 10 00 5A 0A 29
3|1|367 ⊡ ‹408› F0 00 00 0E 0E 00 11 00 4E 18 03
3|2|019 ⊡ ‹408› F0 00 00 0E 0E 00 12 00 5A 1E 25
3|2|148 ⊡ ‹408› F0 00 00 0E 0E 00 13 00 5A 6E 00
3|2|280 ⊡ ‹408› F0 00 00 0E 0E 00 14 00 28 48 24
3|2|412 ⊡ ‹408› F0 00 00 0E 0E 00 15 00 48 24 03
3|3|059 ⊡ ‹408› F0 00 00 0E 0E 00 16 00 56 0A 13
3|3|191 ⊡ ‹408› F0 00 00 0E 0E 00 17 00 44 02 19
3|3|323 ⊡ ‹408› F0 00 00 0E 0E 00 18 00 58 4C 5E
```

Data Dump

A MIDI data dump is merely a MIDI data transmission, either from the MIDI device to a sequencer or from a sequencer back to the device. Some manufacturers have set a product-specific specification that transmits system messages on only one channel, but as a rule system exclusive messages typically have no channel assignment. So, if you're daisy chaining synths together, all synths and sound modules connected together to a single MIDI output will receive the entire sys ex dump. This usually isn't a problem if all the modules and synths are made by separate manufacturers because they shouldn't recognize each other's specific data. If you have two or three synths from the same manufacturer connected in a daisy chain to one MIDI out port, they'll all receive the sys ex information, no matter what MIDI channel they're assigned to! If you don't want them all set exactly the same, this is a big problem. An error in system exclusive transmission could wipe out the programs, layers, presets, and multitimbral combinations in one or more of your sound modules!

The multicable MIDI interface helps this problem because information can be sent through only one cable to a single module, with no daisy chaining involved. With this kind of setup, there shouldn't be any problem transmitting sys ex information because the data is only sent to the module on the assigned MIDI port.

If you have a large daisy chain set up, you might need to connect your modules one at a time for a system exclusive data dump, reconnecting the daisy chain only when all units' system exclusive transmissions have completed.

The Handshake

Some MIDI devices require a specific handshake message before they'll play, receive, or dump any data stream. If you experience a problem with transmitting and receiving sys ex messages, consult the owners' manual. If your piece of gear requires a handshake message, that message will most likely be noted in the manual under system exclusive messages.

If you're using a computer-based sequencer, you can usually simply enter the handshake message in a system exclusive sequence. Once it's entered and can be transmitted, everything should work well. Keep in mind that the handshake will probably need to be sent to the device before the device will dump to the sequencer. It will also need to be transmitted before the sequencer can dump into the device.

Data Backup

Because system exclusive data transmissions have the potential to wipe out your synth, sound module, processor, or mixer settings, it is a very good idea to always keep a backup of your important system exclusive data for each MIDI instrument. It's a fairly simple procedure to create a system exclusive archival sequence for each MIDI instrument. Name and date the sequence. If applicable, include a reference to the song title in the sequence name. Do whatever it takes to eliminate the guesswork when you need to restore your MIDI gear to a previous configuration.

If by chance you transmit a spurious system exclusive message and one of your MIDI devices locks up or seems to have lost its data, try turning the unit off and then back on again before you break out your backup system sequences. Many devices recall their settings when powered up, or there might be a key combination that restores all default settings upon power up.

Quantizing

Quantizing cleans up inaccuracies in a musical performance. For the purposes of this section you're considering the quantizing of musical notes, but many sequencers offer the ability to quantize many different MIDI parameters.

In the process of quantizing, each note is viewed by the sequencer in relation to a note-value grid. The user specifies whether the grid references quarter notes, sixteenth notes, eighth note triplets, and so on. Each note of the performance is pulled to the closest grid unit. If you play a note just after the third sixteenth note of count three, and your grid is set to sixteenth notes, the sequencer will pull the note exactly to the mathematically correct third sixteenth note of beat three. If you perform a note between two grid units the sequencer will pull the

Quantizing

The process of quantizing pulls each note of a performance to the closest background unit. If you've set the sequencer to quantize to the closest eighth note (like the example below) each note will be drawn to the closest eighth note. Notice the inaccuracy of the beat placements in Example 1—hardly any notes fall directly on the beat. Example 2 has been quantized; notice how each note is perfectly placed on the eighth note grid.

Be careful. If you perform a note between two grid units, the sequencer will pull the note onto the closest grid unit. So, if the performance is too sloppy, the sequencer might pull some notes to the wrong beats.

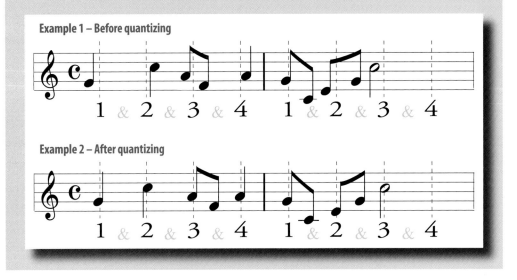

note onto the closest grid unit, so if the performance is too sloppy the sequencer might pull some notes to the wrong beats.

Early-model sequencers popularized the concept of quantizing, sometimes called *auto-correct*. The idea that you could play rhythmically sloppy parts and then have a box make your performance rhythmically perfect was a big hit. The only problem is that nobody really plays rhythmically perfect every time, so the sequencer was soon labeled as mechanical-sounding or machinelike. Because everything was quantized to perfection, there was no emotional personalization.

In reality, music at its best contains plenty of rhythmic imperfections. One artist might be famous for a tendency to produce music that is very intense, often playing ahead of the beat ever so slightly. Another artist might produce a very laid back type of music, demonstrating a tendency to play behind the beat. Good studio musicians need to control beat placement constantly; they know how to create different emotional intensities simply by how they approach the groove. An excellent drummer can adjust beat placement of individual instruments. It's common to hear a drum groove with all of the drums playing right on the beat with the exception of the snare drum, which might be laid back or pushed to create an entirely different feel.

It didn't take sequencer manufacturers long to recognize and address the "feel" issue. Modern sequencers let you adjust levels of quantize in minute detail. Almost anything you can imagine being done to a musical note can be performed quickly and easily. Quantizing is referred to in terms of sensitivity and strength; these days, it's rare to perfectly quantize any part of a sequence unless you're trying to achieve a very mechanical-techno feel.

Strength

Strength is a quantize parameter that determines the degree of perfection attained. Consider that a perfect quantize conforms the notes perfectly to the user-defined grid. The strength of a perfect quantize is 100 percent because it draws the notes 100 percent of the distance toward the grid—all the way. If you set the strength of the quantize to 50 percent, the notes are only drawn half the way to the closest grid value. At 50-percent strength, a note that is 20 percent away from the grid would be drawn to a distance 10 percent away from the grid.

Imagine a magnet, pulling the MIDI notes toward the grid. At 100-percent strength the magnet pulls the notes all the way to the grid.

At 80-percent strength the magnet only pulls the notes 80 percent of the way toward the grid.

Using the strength option is an excellent way to tighten up a musical performance without sterilizing it. I use the strength command on almost all sequenced parts, even if it's just a little bit. On a piano part, adjusting the strength lets you tighten everything in proportion. You can still keep the roll feel of the chords while tightening the groove of the song. I'm an okay keyboardist, but with the right amount of MIDI manipulation I can sound pretty good. Can anybody relate?

Quantize Strength

Strength is a quantize parameter that determines the degree of perfection attained. Imagine a magnet, pulling the MIDI notes toward the grid. At 100-percent strength the magnet pulls the notes all the way to the grid. At 80-percent strength, the magnet only pulls the notes 80 percent of the way toward the grid.

Using the strength option is an excellent way to tighten up a musical performance without sterilizing it.

80-percent strength will pull each of these notes 80 percent of the way to the beat.

Each note has been moved 80 percent closer to the beat.

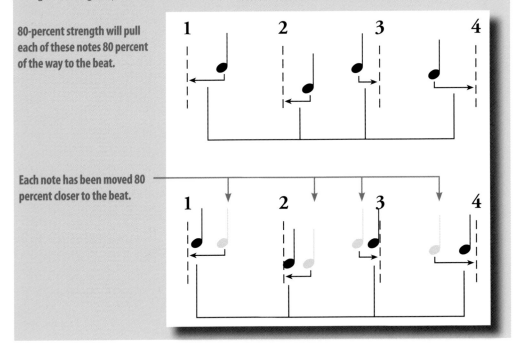

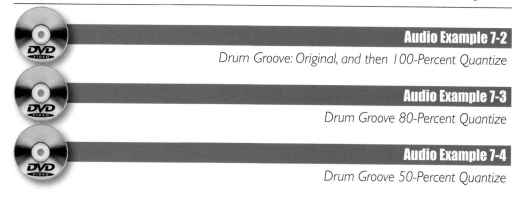

Audio Example 7-2

Drum Groove: Original, and then 100-Percent Quantize

Audio Example 7-3

Drum Groove 80-Percent Quantize

Audio Example 7-4

Drum Groove 50-Percent Quantize

Sensitivity

The sensitivity control adjusts the area that can be quantized. In a lot of rhythmic feels, the notes that are between the beats are very style-driven and they change depending on the emotion of the song. To quantize the notes closest to the grid and leave the notes between the grid alone, you could adjust the sensitivity control on a percentage scale.

At 100-percent sensitivity the area of effect extends continuously between the grid locations. At 50-percent sensitivity the notes in the middle 50 percent between grid locations would not be quantized, while the notes in the area extending 25 percent on either side of the grid would be quantized either perfectly or in relation to the percentage selected in the strength option.

The sensitivity option also allows for quantizing only the notes between the grid locations. Negative numbers tell the processor to quantize in relation to the center point between grid locations. So, a negative-50-percent sensitivity leaves the notes that surround the grid (25 percent on either side) alone, while quantizing the notes that surround the center point between grid locations (25 percent on either side) according to the grid and strength settings.

Audio Example 7-5

Reference Groove

Quantize Sensitivity

At 50-percent sensitivity (as in the illustration below), the notes in the middle 50 percent between grid locations will not be quantized, while the notes in the area extending 25 percent on either side of the grid will be quantized—either perfectly or in relation to the percentage selected in the strength option.

Negative numbers tell the processor to quantize in relation to the center point between grid locations. Therefore, a –50 percent sensitivity leaves the notes that surround the background unit grid alone (25 percent on either side), while quantizing the notes that surround the center point between grid locations (25 percent on either side) according to the background unit and strength settings.

100-percent sensitivity quantizes everything between the user-set background unit.

50-percent sensitivity only quantizes notes in a range that is half the width of the background unit, centered on the beat.

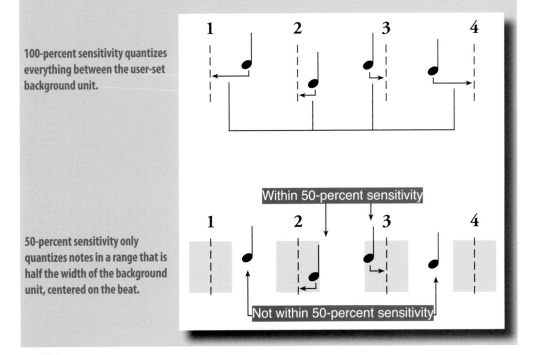

Audio Example 7-6

50-Percent Sensitivity

Audio Example 7-7

Negative 50-Percent Sensitivity

When these features are used in a musical way, the effect is a very real, precise, and lifelike sequence. The primary problem with 100-percent quantizing lies in the hiding of notes. If all notes are lined up perfectly on the beat, the brain doesn't have time to recognize the individual ingredients. Once the parts are spread out in a more realistic way, it's amazing how much more fun the sequence is.

In Audio Example 7-8, notice how the track comes to life when it is only partially quantized.

Audio Example 7-8

Absolute, and then Partial Quantize

Absolute versus Partial Quantizing

The primary problem with 100-percent quantizing lies in the hiding of notes. If all notes are lined up perfectly on the beat, the brain doesn't have time to recognize the individual ingredients. Once the parts are spread out in a more realistic way, it's amazing how much more fun the sequence is to listen to.

Notice in Example 1 how the notes lay on top of each other. The instruments are all fighting for visibility. In Example 2 each note is more realistically spread out around the beat and is, therefore, much easier to hear and recognize. This simple concept explains why sequences often sound sterile, lacking personality and impact.

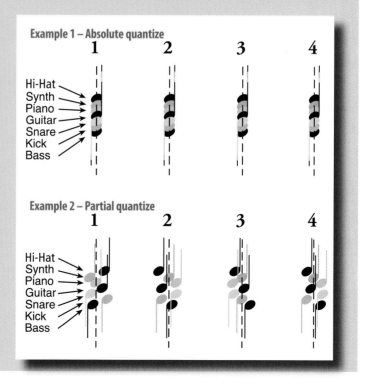

Example 1 – Absolute quantize
1   2   3   4

Hi-Hat
Synth
Piano
Guitar
Snare
Kick
Bass

Example 2 – Partial quantize
1   2   3   4

Hi-Hat
Synth
Piano
Guitar
Snare
Kick
Bass

How Tight Is Tight Enough?

Once you're in the "let's make it perfect" mode, it's difficult to know when to turn back. How perfect is good enough and how loose is loose enough? Good, objective decisions regarding the appropriate feel only come from being fully immersed in the style you're recording. Refer to recordings of live musicians in the style you're recording. Some vintage recordings are downright sloppy at times. Was this because it was stylistically correct, or was it because the players weren't capable of executing their parts? The '50s and '60s were an era of growth in R&B and rock. Folks with passion and vision but not a lot of refinement laid down many of the roots. At the same time, the jazz and big-band genres were becoming quite sophisticated; not only were the players totally into their styles, but the art had grown to a high performance level. Some of the jazz recordings from that era were full of artistic genius. However, early rock and R&B music was full of life—those recordings mark a peak of inspiration and innovation.

Some of the Steely Dan recordings or Toto's efforts were phenomenal from a musical, artistic, and technical viewpoint. These works represent great musicians performing at an amazingly proficient level. The performances were always right in the pocket; it would be tough to find anything that seems rhythmically or melodically misplaced, yet there is life, energy, and personality. Many current recordings retain those same qualities—and yes, even a sequenced song can sound full of life.

I try to quantize so the parts feel great; sometimes that means 50 percent, other times 95 percent, and still others 0 percent. Use the tools available to bring out the life of the music. I've seen young producers intentionally leave a very sloppy performance in a sequence in an attempt provide life. In reality, the sloppiness can become a distraction, especially when it's outside the boundaries of tolerance for live performance.

Technology has given us nearly complete control over musical performances. Nowadays, the recordist can be blamed as much for a sloppy performance as the artist. However, even with the nearly complete control available in recording, it's important to understand that recording decisions must be based on musical grounds, not on binary hexadecimal codes.

Randomize

Randomize is the opposite of quantize. This feature represents the attempt to put some human feel back into a previously quantized sequence. If you're provided a sequence that has been put together on a low-end sequencer that doesn't offer the sophisticated controls mentioned herein, or one that has been constructed by someone with a lack of understanding in this area, randomizing could be your key to success.

Randomizing is also referred to in percentages, like sensitivity and strength. One-hundred-percent randomizing results in repositioning of the notes anywhere within the range of 50 percent on either side of the grid. In most cases, this degree of randomizing creates rhythmic pandemonium. However, when randomizing to smaller percentages, an otherwise sterile sequence can regain life and impact.

In Audio Examples 7-9 through 7-11 the background unit is based on sixteenth notes. Notice the difference in feel between the perfectly quantized Audio Example 7-9 and the randomized examples.

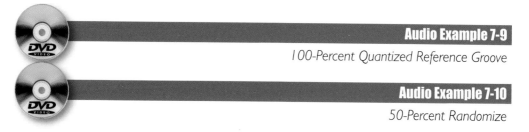

Audio Example 7-9

100-Percent Quantized Reference Groove

Audio Example 7-10

50-Percent Randomize

Randomizing

Randomizing is also referred to in percentages, like sensitivity and strength. 100-percent randomizing results in the repositioning of the notes anywhere within the range of 50-percent on either side of the grid. In most cases, this degree of randomizing creates rhythmic pandemonium. However, when randomizing to smaller percentages, an otherwise sterile sequence can regain life and impact.

Although the effect of random- izing looks much like partial quantizing on paper, it doesn't usually provide the same kind of rhythmic feel. Partial quantizing retains the rhythmic tendency of each musical part. If one part tends to push the groove when originally recorded, partial quantizing tightens up the "personality" of the part. Randomizing, on the other hand, simply places notes randomly around the background unit without regard to feel or rhythmic tendencies.

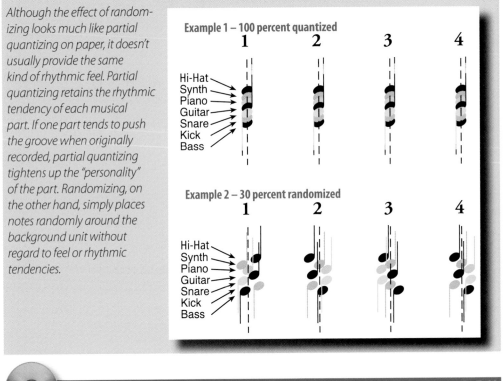

Example 1 – 100 percent quantized

Example 2 – 30 percent randomized

Audio Example 7-11

10-Percent Randomize

Real Time

Real-time recording in the MIDI world is a totally relative concept. In concept, the MIDI information is recorded without being quantized, but the drawback is the resolution of the MIDI clock. The early MIDI sequencers only had resolutions of 24 or 48 units per quarter note. That resolution is nowhere near fine enough to render a realistic real-time recording. The results were always very choppy and uncomfortable.

Audio Example 7-12

Original Performance without Sequencer

Audio Example 7-13

Real-Time Sequence of Audio Example 7–12 at 24 Pulses per Quarter Note (ppq)

The only way to beat the real-time resolution game was to set the sequencer so it didn't quantize, while adjusting the tempo to its fastest setting. If your song tempo was 70 quarter notes per minute but the tempo was set to 210 quarter notes per minute, the resolution would be increased by a factor of three. Therefore, if your original resolution was 24 units per beat, the new resolution would effectively be 72 units per beat—not good, but definitely better. This was a bit of a cheesy fix, but it helped as long as the sequence data didn't create a bottleneck at the accelerated tempo setting.

With the growth of the computer-based sequencer, we started to see the MIDI clock resolution increase. Most modern sequencers offer resolutions of 480 or even 960 units per quarter note. These increased resolutions offer a much more realistic-sounding real-time recording, although complete capture of the musical interpretation is still debatable.

Audio Example 7-14

Original Performance without Sequencer

Audio Example 7-15

Real-Time Sequence of Audio Example 7–14 at 480 ppq

Audio Example 7-16

Original Performance without Sequencer

Audio Example 7-17

Real-Time Sequence of Audio Example 7–16 at 960 ppq

Step Record

Step recording is simply a means of recording a rhythmic part one note at a time. The grid and note values are determined ahead of time. If you determine the note value to be sixteenth notes you can play the notes or chords in order, but they don't need to be in rhythm. There is typically a set of computer keyboard commands to speed up the process. When you press the key command for quarter notes, whatever notes you play from then on will have a quarter-note value. Once you press the key command for eighth notes, the notes you play will be eighth notes, and so on. You can determine any note or tuplet value.

Step recording is most useful as a tool to compensate for a lack of performance proficiency. Every once in a while a musical part calls out to be included, but it's a little too difficult to actually play into the sequence, even if you slow the tempo way down. Simply figure out the notes and rhythm, and then step record it into the sequence. When you play the sequence back at the correct tempo, you'll probably be amazed at how impressive the part sounds.

The main drawback to step recording is that every note is 100-percent quantized, and they're usually all the same volume, velocity, and expression. Randomizing after the fact or adjusting some of the note velocities can help revitalize an otherwise sterile step-recorded part.

Be careful that the musical parts you create through step-record mode are believable. It's a natural tendency to create lines that are too fast or too harmonically dense. Parts such as these might be acceptable as an effect when used sparingly, but they usually distract more than they enhance.

Audio Example 7-18

Unrealistic Step Recording

Shifting Tracks

Because MIDI values are simply binary codes referenced to a time clock, it has become commonplace to move tracks, notes, and segments. The shift feature is a boon to the process of creating a specific musical feel. If an ingredient needs to feel aggressive and on edge, shift it forward slightly in relation to the rest of the sequence. If an ingredient needs to feel more relaxed, delay it slightly. It's effective when building a drum and percussion track to shift certain ingredients to lend the appropriate emotional feel and support to the music. The snare track is often shifted forward in time to help the momentum of the drum track.

Audio Example 7-19

Reference Groove

Audio Example 7-20

Snare Drum Shifted Forward

Listen to Audio Examples 7-21 and 7-22. Audio Example 7-21 has been quantized to 95-percent strength with no tracks shifted. Audio Example 7-22 has some tracks shifted in either direction to help add life. See whether you can tell which tracks were moved and which direction they were moved. Notice the difference in the emotional feel of each example.

Audio Example 7-21

Reference Groove 95-Percent Quantized

Audio Example 7-22

Audio Example 7–21 with Tracks Shifted

Velocities, Durations, and Tempos

Velocities, durations, tempos, and many other musical aspects are completely controllable and moldable through MIDI manipulation.

Each sequencer handles adjustments of these parameters in its own way, but the concepts are typically identical. Once you begin to understand the basics of these controls, the details fall painlessly into place. You should be able to cross between hardware and software sequencers with a minimal amount of adjustment, primarily because you'll know what to expect—you'll know what to look for.

Many terms common to analog signal processing have been adopted by MIDI program developers. Most programs give you the option to create delays, compression, echoes, arpeggios, choruses, and more. The controls have come to resemble a piece of hardware rather than a box full of numbers.

Strings and Pads

When you hear a string pad that sounds rich, full, and very interesting, the appeal isn't always the result of an incredible raw sound. What's been done with the sound is often the most impressive part.

Layering

One technique that consistently produces good, interesting sounds is layering. *Layering* is a common keyboard term that refers to the process of stacking one sound on top of another. Within the keyboard, layering is done by assigning two or more internal sounds to play at once, every time you hit a key. This works so well because as the two basic sounds interact, the harmonics and overtones combine. Rather than continually shaping one sound to achieve just the right sound, find two separate sounds that each contain part of what you need, and then play them together.

One of the ways you can create interesting new sounds that no one has heard before is by layering one keyboard with a different keyboard. The chances of someone creating the exact sound you've found—combining a Triton with a QS-8, for instance—aren't nearly as likely as if you'd layered two of the standard internal QS-8 sounds. Take advantage of the tools that are available to you. Just because a keyboard isn't the newest piece of technology on the block doesn't mean it won't sound great with another keyboard or sound module.

Listen to the two fairly plain and simple string sounds in Audio Example 7-23. I play the parts separately, and then I layer them together. Notice how they take on a much more rich and interesting character when they're heard together than when they're heard separately.

Audio Example 7-23
Layering

If there are enough tracks or channels available, pan the two keyboards slightly apart to simulate a wider "section" sound, as in Audio Example 7-24.

Audio Example 7-24
Panning the Layered Sounds Apart

A common technique when layering sounds is to slightly detune the sounds. This accentuates the harmonic interaction between the two sounds, creating a larger overall feel. This technique has the potential to be extreme because you're layering two different sounds rather than simply running one sound through the harmonizer.

In Audio Example 7-25, I'll slightly detune the two different string sounds. One keyboard is tuned eight cents sharp and the other is tuned eight cents flat. If your keyboard doesn't have a tuner that indicates tuning by cents, try using a guitar tuner; most guitar tuners show tuning in cents. I'll add these sounds one at a time, pan them apart, and then pan them together to center.

The technique of layering can be carried as far as your mixer, tracks, and available keyboards will allow. Although you can reach a point where simply adding one more keyboard sound doesn't make much of a difference, it is common to use two, three, or even four keyboards playing the identical part to shape an interesting, unique sound.

Use each keyboard or sound module for a specific part of the overall sound you're building. Samplers often help to add realism. If a very intimate sampled string sound—including the sound of the bow scraping across the strings—is combined with a very full, lush pad, the result is usually very impressive and full.

In Audio Example 7-26, I combine three elements: the bright, sampled single-string sound; the large, defined string pad; and the mellow, filling, smooth string pad. I play each sound separately and then combine them. Finally, I vary their pan placement. Notice how the sum of all these parts sounds much better—and more interesting—than any of the individual pieces.

Notation Software

Most computer-based sequencing packages offer a music notation view of the individual parts. This is a very convenient and powerful tool for those who think in terms of traditional music notation. However, if you want to print parts for the rhythm section, string section, woodwind section, or the horn section, invest in a high-quality notation software package. These packages are able to produce professional-looking musical parts, and, once you get the hang of the program, they are timesavers. Be prepared to invest a fair amount of time into learning the program.

Uses

At first, you'll probably feel like you'd be better off using hand manuscript—that is, until you need to transpose the entire arrangement because the key you selected didn't work. Transpositions are a snap with a notation package. The chord symbols typically transpose just as easily as notes. This is a great feature for creating parts for a trumpet, sax, or other transposing instrument. The software does all the instrument transpositions automatically. In addition, it points out any rhythmic and instrument range errors.

Notation can be entered from the computer keyboard or played in through a MIDI device. The ability to play the musical parts from a keyboard is a huge timesaver, especially over hand manuscript. Once the parts are in the notation software, you can play them back through MIDI to verify their accuracy. As an arranger, it's very valuable to hear your music before you hand the parts to the players!

Lyrics

Most notation packages let you type lyrics into a lyric sheet, and then the computer simply scrolls the lyrics under the notes. The software compensates for ties, rests, and slurs. This is one of the most useful functions when you are preparing a lead sheet or backing vocal part—and it looks cool, too.

Chord Symbols

Chord symbols are a necessity for rhythm section parts and lead sheets. Notation software typically lets you simply play the chord in on a keyboard. The chords are recognized and entered with minimal effort.

Lead Sheet

The lyrics in this lead sheet were automatically scrolled under the notes. The software recognizes and adjusts for rests, ties, and slurs. In this software package, the chord symbols are harmonically related to the melody and they transpose automatically, along with any key change.

Notation software provides printed music that is easy-to-read, instantly transposed, and simple to update.

You can also make up your own chord library so software will recognize your voicings and accurately label the harmonies.

Brass, Woodwinds, and Strings

The best way to structure brass, woodwinds, and strings is to thoughtfully and intentionally map them out before they're performed. If you're hiring musicians, it's fairly obvious that you better have well-written charts for them that are easy to read and follow. However, even when you're playing the parts on a synth, your musical impact will be greatly increased if you structure all of the parts before you perform them.

Notation software offers a huge bonus anytime you're creating orchestrations that contain live musicians playing brass, woodwinds, or strings. It's simple to set a MIDI sound module to simulate the sounds of each instrument as you structure each ingredient. Today it is no problem to hear all parts together before you're paying hourly for each musician in an expensive commercial recording facility—you'll only truly appreciate this feature if you've ever had to sleuth out poor written or copied manuscript in the same situation. Can you feel the pain in my words?

Many notation software manufacturers have either cut back their focus on these programs or have, in some cases, ceased production. With recent musical trends, fewer new musicians are traditionally schooled; therefore, reading standard notation is less common than it was ten or twenty years ago. If you're feeling the desire to learn more about music theory and notation, I recommend you go for it. A greater understanding of music fundamentals provides a greater foundation for musical decisions. Also, the more you understand traditional musical rules, the better you're insight into how best to break them. I am very thankful for three aspects of my musical career: 1.) I received an excellent traditional education. 2.) I've always had other like-minded friends to experiment with musically. 3.) I started recording at a healthy time in the analog era, which provided the perspective to greatly appreciate what was technologically and musically good about that era, along with the experience to appreciate what is great about the modern technological and musical era.

Education is good!

Mixing with MIDI

Especially with the onset of the combination digital audio/MIDI sequencer, all mixing and effects can be performed within the boundaries of your computer. Many home and studio recordists have sold their large recording consoles in favor of small, fairly simple mixers.

Parameters

It's common to perform all mixing and effects tasks on the computer while sending a stereo signal to the mixer for monitoring purposes only. In the final mixdown, you might bypass the mixer altogether, sending a digital signal out of the computer into the digital input of a DAT, CD, DVD, or other digital recording platform.

Not only do you have access to all parameters imaginable through MIDI, but they can also all be automated. By the time the mix is ready to print, all the levels, pans, mutes, equalizations, and fades are happening automatically—all you have to do is sit back and enjoy the moment.

Combining MIDI Mix Tools

Amazing power comes from the combination of a digital recording/ sequencing package and a digital recording console. Prices on this gear have dropped dramatically in past years. Because of technological advances, recouping of development costs, and good old-fashioned competition, we can all at least have a shot at owning many of these tools. In many ways, I can do more at my home studio now than I could at any studio in the world not too long ago! The one thing most of us can't replace at home, however, is well-designed acoustical space. Professional studios offer recording environments that are full of excitement and inspiration. All you need to do is clap your hands once in a large, impeccably put-together studio and you immediately understand.

Synthetic reverberation can't replace the open sound of a recording in an excellent studio.

General MIDI Specifications

In 1991, manufacturers agreed to a specific set of MIDI standards called General MIDI (GM). GM standardizes locations and MIDI channels for synths and sound modules, allowing musicians to share sequencing work with some assurance that their sequences can be played back easily.

GM synthesizers support all 16 MIDI channels and offer at least 24-voice polyphony and 16-voice multitimbral output, for a minimum of one voice available for each MIDI channel. Percussion parts are always on MIDI channel 10, using a minimum set of 47 standard drum and percussion sounds mapped according to the GM standard.

All 128 program sounds are defined by their type and patch location. Even though sound modules vary substantially in their sound

General MIDI Drum Sound Map

MIDI Note #	GM Drum Sound	MIDI Note #	GM Drum Sound	MIDI Note #	GM Drum Sound
35	Acoustic Bass Drum	51	Ride Cymbal	67	High Agogo
36	Bass Drum 1	52	Chinese Cymbal	68	Low Agogo
37	Side Stick	53	Ride Bell	69	Cabasa
38	Acoustic Snare	54	Tambourine	70	Maracas
39	Hand Clap	55	Splash Cymbal	71	Short Whistle
40	Electric Snare	56	Cowbell	72	Long Whistle
41	Low Floor Tom	57	Crash Cymbal 2	73	Short Guiro
42	Closed Hi-Hat	58	Vibraslap	74	Long Guiro
43	High Floor Tom	59	Ride Cybmal 2	75	Claves
44	Pedal Hi-Hat	60	High Bongo	76	High Woodblock
45	Low Tom	61	Low Bongo	77	Low Woodblock
46	Open Hi-Hat	62	Mute High Conga	78	Mute Cuica
47	Low Mid Tom	63	Open High Conga	79	Open Cuica
48	High Mid Tom	64	Low Conga	80	Mute Triangle
49	Crash Cymbal	65	High Timbale	81	Open Triangle
50	High Tom	66	Low Timbale		

General MIDI Voices

Prg #	GM Voice	Prg #	GM Voice	Prg #	GM Voice
1	Acoustic Grand	44	Contrabass	87	Lead 7 (Fifths)
2	Bright Acoustic Piano	45	Tremelo Strings	88	Lead 8 (Bass + Lead)
3	Electric Grand Piano	46	Pizzicato Strings	89	Pad 1 (New Age)
4	Honky-Tonk Piano	47	Orchestral Harp	90	Pad 2 (Warm)
5	Electric Piano 1	48	Timpani	91	Pad 3 (Polysynth)
6	Electric Piano 2	49	String Ensemble 1	92	Pad 4 (Choir)
7	Harpsichord	50	String Ensemble 2	93	Pad 5 (Bowed)
8	Clavinet	51	SynthStrings 1	94	Pad 6 (Metallic)
9	Celesta	52	SynthStrings 2	95	Pad 7 (Halo)
10	Glockenspiel	53	Choir Aahs	96	Pad 8 (Sweep)
11	Music Box	54	Voice Oohs	97	FX 1 (Rain)
12	Vibraphone	55	Synth Voice	98	FX 2 (Soundtrack)
13	Marimba	56	Orchestra Hits	99	FX 3 (Crystal)
14	Xylophone	57	Trumpet	100	FX 4 (Atmosphere)
15	Tubular Bells	58	Trombone	101	FX 5 (Brightness)
16	Dulcimer	59	Tuba	102	FX 6 (Goblins)
17	Drawbar Organ	60	Muted Trumpet	103	FX 7 (Echoes)
18	Percussive Organ	61	French Horn	104	FX 8 (Sci-Fi)
19	Rock Organ	62	Brass Section	105	Sitar
20	Church Organ	63	SynthBrass 1	106	Banjo
21	Reed Organ	64	SynthBrass 2	107	Shamisen
22	Accordian	65	Soprano Sax	108	Koto
23	Harmonica	66	Alto Sax	109	Kalimba
24	Tango Accordian	67	Tenor Sax	110	Bagpipe
25	Acoustic Guitar (Nylon)	68	Baritone Sax	111	Fiddle
26	Acoustic Guitar (Steel)	69	Oboe	112	Shanai
27	Electric Guitar (Jazz)	70	English Horn	113	Tinkle Bell
28	Electric Guitar (Clean)	71	Bassoon	114	Agogo
29	Electric Guitar (Muted)	72	Clarinet	115	Steel Drum
30	Overdriven Guitar	73	Piccolo	116	Woodblock
31	Distortion Guitar	74	Flute	117	Taiko Drum
32	Guitar Harmonics	75	Recorder	118	Melodic Tom
33	Acoustic Bass	76	Pan Flute	119	Synth Drum
34	Electric Bass (Finger)	77	Blown Bottle	120	Reverse Cymbal
35	Electric Bass (Pick)	78	Shakuhachi	121	Guitar Fret Noise
36	Fretless Bass	79	Whistle	122	Breath Noise
37	Slap Bass 1	80	Ocarina	123	Seashore
38	Slap Bass 2	81	Lead 1 (Square)	124	Bird Tweet
39	Synth Bass 1	82	Lead 2 (Sawtooth)	125	Telephone Ring
40	Synth Bass 2	83	Lead 3 (Calliope)	126	Helicopter
41	Violin	84	Lead 4 (Chiff)	127	Applause
42	Viola	85	Lead 5 (Charang)	128	Gunshot
43	Cello	86	Lead 6 (Voice)		

quality and subjective appeal, the General MIDI standard is still very effective in its ability to coordinate an otherwise disjointed and separated segment of the music industry. It's very convenient for publishers and songwriters to distribute MIDI files with some assurance that they'll make musical sense on playback. It provides a means to share or sell MIDI tracks that can be edited and customized by the recipient.

General MIDI devices all respond to the same set of controllers, with predetermined and standardized ranges for each. GM devices need to respond in like manner to pitch bend, velocity, aftertouch, master tuning, reset all controllers, and all notes off commands.

Standard MIDI File

With so many types of sequencers and software packages available for MIDI sequencing, the MIDI music industry made a mature decision a number of years ago to create a standardized format that could be read by any MIDI sequencer. Sometimes track names or other visual formats are lost in translation, but at the very least all notes and control parameters remain intact whenever a standard MIDI file is saved from one sequencer and then opened in another.

Cross-Platform Compatibility

The standard MIDI file is an excellent transition format between your MIDI sequencer and notation software. It's typical to record a sequence in the sequencer software first to determine the arrangement and orchestration, and to later save a copy in standard MIDI file format. The standard MIDI file then opens up splendidly from your music notation software, where the lyrics and print refinements are added to create a professional-looking piece of music.

There are also very useful applications for beginning your song in the notation package. This approach lets you refine any instrumental arrangements and orchestrations, transferring them through the standard MIDI file to the sequencer once they're perfected. Files that are begun in a notation package are typically quantized to 100 percent, so you might need to use the available sequencer functions to randomize, humanize, and generally spruce up the sequence.

Keyboard and Mix Controllers

The hub of any extensive MIDI system is the keyboard or mix controller. The only space-efficient way to set up a MIDI menagerie is to revolve several MIDI devices around a central controller that can access all MIDI parameters in a simple and quick way.

Keyboard Controllers

The master keyboard controller for a MIDI system might or might not have a sound module built in. Many controllers simply act as a keyboard to send MIDI signals to sound modules. Often the master keyboard also has sound generators built in, but to be an effective master controller it should be able to divide into separate regions that can simultaneously drive different MIDI channels and sound modules.

A good master keyboard controller lets you set up presets to instantaneously switch all sound modules to predetermined patches and controller settings.

A separate master controller gives the performer the ability to select an actual keyboard size, design, and action that remains constant no matter what sound module is being driven. Most pianists prefer a natural-feeling 88-key weighted action. They just play better in that kind of performance environment, especially when they're playing piano-like musical parts. Some keyboardists prefer a typical plastic non-weighted keyboard when performing organ, strings, brass, or other synthesized electronic sounds; the action is more conducive to the correct stylistic interpretation of these types of musical ingredients.

Mix Controllers

In the digital recording arena, although all options can be controlled onscreen within the computer or hardware, there's still a place for actually controlling the signal with a physical knob, fader, or button.

Keyboard Controller

A good MIDI controller keyboard can divide into multiple user-selectable zones. Each zone can be sent to its own MIDI channel or device, thereby facilitating easy and quick access to many sounds. Sounds can also be easily layered on a controller keyboard.

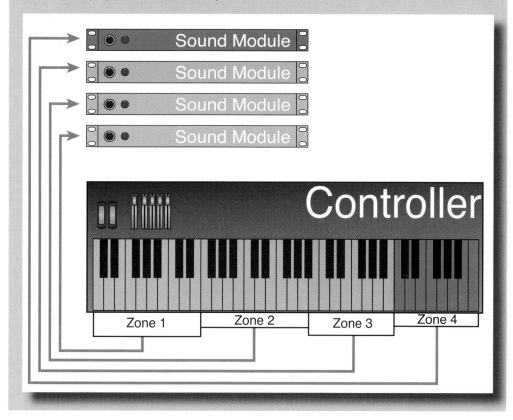

Several companies offer hardware control surfaces for interfacing with some amazing software packages.

Most mix controllers contain a minimum number of channels (typically eight) but offer a maximum amount of control. Each channel can be assigned to access any number of channels and parameters—the exact number depends on the extent of the digital audio hardware and software. This type of interface offers the ability to actually touch something that feels like a regular console to change a level, pan, aux send, EQ, and so on. Along with these tactile mixing and editing capabilities, most controllers provide transport control, moving faders, meters, various windows that read and track the status of any selected parameter, and options for expandability to as many faders and knobs as your needs demand.

Most of these controllers use the same MIDI language for parameter control that is used by synthesizers and sound modules. Some manufacturers address the zipper effect (audible stair-stepping through the 128 MIDI parameter levels) by combining two or more MIDI controller numbers for one function. For example, the stereo master fader really should combine at least two MIDI controller parameters in a way that doubles the resolution of the stair steps to 256 discrete levels. Because a fade out at the end of a song can take 10 or more seconds, there is ample opportunity to hear the zipper effect at work. Different manufacturers address this problem in different ways, but most serious audio companies design solutions to minimize this effect.

I've worked on small digital mixers with very few faders and one access window, and I've worked on larger surfaces with instant access through faders, buttons, and knobs. Although the digital system allows for a minimal control surface for many channels and parameters, the more efficient systems are set up much like a regular 24-channel mixer. Integration of a computer monitor with the physical mixer provides the best of both worlds: tactile controls and ease of use through the visual onscreen interface.

MIDI Machine Control (MMC)

MIDI Machine Control uses specific MIDI commands for controlling transport and cueing functions. Most modern recorders, such as those made by Alesis, Tascam, Sony, Fostex, Otari, and so on, can be controlled through MMC. These machines must be connected to the MIDI controller through standard MIDI cables and an interface. The specific controller could be a software-based sequencing/digital audio package, a dedicated hardware controller, or a master tape machine.

Whether hardware- or software-based, MMC controls look and act like tape-deck-style transport controls. In a typical setup, the MMC controller sends transport commands to another MMC device, which serves as an address master. The address master generates and distributes time-code information to all recording and playback devices, which in turn chase and lock according to the MMC commands. It's not necessary that post-address master devices and machines respond to MMC commands; they must simply follow the timing commands supplied by the address master.

MIDI System Design: What Should I Have?

Let's review some MIDI abilities, capabilities, and musical applications while we map out a potential MIDI system.

Synths

We often think of a synth as a self-contained sound generating keyboard. Modern "synthesizers" often provide excellent controller functions, sound module features, sampling capacity, and effects processing. As you build your system consider the status of current technology, and avoid duplicating functions with redundant gear. Choose redundancy when it increases your audio quality, or when it increases your efficiency.

Controller

It's necessary to have a master keyboard to access and perform the myriad sounds available in the MIDI world. You can include a dedicated MIDI controller in your system, which contains no sound-generating capabilities. These controllers offer quick and easy access to all MIDI parameter controls as well as simple routines for layering and splitting MIDI channels, devices, and sound modules. Often controllers are purchased because of the type of keys they provide. Whether weighted keys, such as the kind on an acoustic piano, or plastic unweighted keys, such as the type on many synthesizers, a dedicated controller gives the artist a consistent keyboard action and feel.

Most modern MIDI keyboards contain ample control to perform well as controllers for all devices in your system. In fact, many artists include an excellent 88-weighted-key synth, on which they love the sounds, and a 76-key unweighted key synth in their systems. Either keyboard can act as the controller, at the performer's discretion. Traditional pianists prefer the feel of weighted keys, just like the ones on an excellent grand piano. However, any experienced player knows the importance of light plastic keys to the performance of most B-3 organ licks, in addition to many other sounds that demand a light action for proper performance.

If there is a computer involved in a system in which the controllers also generate sounds, simply enter the Global control mode and disable local control. This way, all MIDI signals are sent to the computer and then routed back to the sound generator or to any other device in the system. The controller keyboard won't make a sound unless it is connected properly via the MIDI network.

Sound Modules

Once you've chosen a master controller, it's fun, easy, and inexpensive to add sound modules. Every good synth comes in a rack-mountable version at a significantly reduced price. If you already have a sequencer and a controller, you can often save 50 percent off the keyboard/ workstation by simply purchasing the module. It's easier to keep up with current sounds when you only need the scaled-down sound module.

Sequencers

A sequencer records and manipulates MIDI data. When sequencers originally appeared on the musical scene they revolutionized music production, sometimes to the point where every sound was generated from a sound module and performed through MIDI—the keyboardist's paradise. Guitar, bass, and drums were in danger of pop-music extinction. Then, one day the music industry realized that real instruments were pretty cool after all and order was restored to the universe.

Hence, modern sequencers are almost always combined with digital recording capabilities and are easily interconnected with most audio and video playback and recording systems. We now take advantage of all that MIDI offers, plus we record audio in the same working environment. To make it even better, modern recording software provides most of the same types of editing and data-control features over audio recordings that got everybody excited about MIDI.

Hardware Black Boxes

Some hardware sequencers that are sold as freestanding units offer many professional features. They're usually cheaper than the cost of a computer and a software package (especially if you include the cost of a good multicable MIDI interface), and they require no computer. However, they're more cumbersome, confusing, and time consuming to operate. Black boxes are appealing because they're typically designed from the ground up with accurate sequence timing in mind. They don't share a processor with any other computer function. They're often the most constant in reference to the groove.

Computer Software Packages

If it's at all financially possible, buy a computer and the best software package available. Almost everyone already has the computer, but even if you need to purchase one, this route will probably be much less expensive in the long run. Most users soon feel the frustration of a hardware sequencer (with one or two small access windows and a maze of pages to scroll through). It's often difficult to perform even basic MIDI functions with these hardware-based systems. These boxes frequently are sold for a fraction of what they originally cost in order to get into a computer-based system.

When it comes time to buy, check out catalogs and music stores. You'll soon find what's hot and what's not. Consider that although the prices through mail order might be cheaper (and you might be able to dodge taxation), there will be a time when you need help—and quickly. At those times, you'll certainly appreciate the concept of a local, friendly, knowledgeable, helpful salesperson who is willing to give you on-the-spot support. If you're talking to a dealer who seems to have little or no knowledge of the product, buy elsewhere.

Interfaces

The type of MIDI interface you include in your system should match your current needs while at the same time addressing your musical future . If you're a keyboardist with a few sound modules, a controller, and aspirations for greatness, don't underestimate your needs. Buy a powerful interface that is expandable and which addresses musical, recording, audio, and video needs.

Simple Interface

If you have a small MIDI setup and you don't expect it to grow much, buy an inexpensive interface. These interfaces typically provide one or two MIDI inputs that split to a few MIDI outputs. This is perfectly appropriate for many simple setups.

Multicable Interface

If you have several sound modules and you see growth in your future, don't waste time or money on anything other than a good multicable interface that reads and writes time code, with provision for further expansion.

These interfaces typically offer eight MIDI cable inputs and outputs. Each cable connection offers a complete set of all 16 MIDI channels. Therefore, with eight cables, each containing 16 MIDI channels, the complete interface provides control of 128 discrete MIDI channels.

In addition to offering control of an impressive number of channels, these interfaces typically link together to provide hundreds or even thousands of MIDI channels. Although this might seem excessive on the surface, consider that each sound module offers separate control and access to all 16 MIDI channels. A system with 10 MIDI devices could require 160 MIDI channels for complete multitimbral control.

Additionally, don't forget that this interface is your link to the audio and video post-production world. If you have goals that include film scoring and audio for video composition, you must have an interface that follows and generates SMPTE time code, and chases and provides word clock sync and MTC machine control data, while generating and chasing control information for ADAT sync, Sony 9-pin sync, and more. This is an important part of a modern system.

Word Clock Hubs

As the prevalence of digital devices has exploded in recent years, word clock stability throughout the digital system has become increasingly crucial. It is best in a large MIDI/digital audio system to include a very stable and well-respected word clock generator that simultaneously drives all digital devices. An excellent work clock source increases the system stability, while at the same time solidifying the audio data stream. In other words, it makes your recordings sound better.

Mixers

Whether analog or digital, there is a good chance that your modern mixer provides some interface with the MIDI world. Trends in music seem to flow between technologically influenced music and more unplugged, traditional musically influenced music. However, MIDI and the control it brings is an important agreement in your mixing experience, whether 100 percent into techno music or 100 percent into bluegrass music.

Digital Mixer

Digital mixers have become very affordable and offer tons of features, plus total automation. You can't go too far off base in this arena. But it's always important to test the mixer before you buy. The sound quality on digital mixers is usually good, but some have a grainy kind of a zing-like sound. As with any audio equipment, always listen before you buy. A manufacturer can tout features and sound quality 'til the cows come home, but we should all make a stand to base our purchasing decisions on sound quality, ease of use, and musicality. We are, after all, dealing with music first and technology second.

Analog Mixers with MIDI Control

Most modern analog mixers offer MIDI-controlled mutes at the very least. There's usually a set of MIDI ports on the console; just plug into your MIDI network, open the manual, and start amazing yourself with the possibilities for creative freedom.

MIDI-Controlled Automation

There are several MIDI-controlled automation systems available. They typically have external hardware that intercepts all mixer outputs, inserting a VCA in each channel that allows for automated fader and mute control. These packages are very powerful aids in the mixing process, but they don't offer the complete control offered by a fully digital mixer.

Digital Audio Cards

If you're using a computer-based sequencer, I highly recommend upgrading to a combined MIDI/digital audio package. You might or might not need to add an audio card to your computer, depending on your computer format and audio needs. The power and flexibility of housing your MIDI sequence and live audio recording in the same box is incredible. You can cut, paste, copy, and undo all audio segments in the same manner as MIDI data, and everything is on one screen. Mixing digital audio and MIDI instruments is all done on the same computer screen. It's the best way to work that I've found so far, and, when run in tandem with a digital mixer, it offers phenomenal creative freedom.

Combining MIDI Sequencing and Digital Audio

Modern digital audio cards very vastly in their capabilities. Bit depth and sample rate specifications determine the limit of your audio quality and compatibility with modern formats. When you're purchasing a digital audio card or interface, research the device in your target price range that provides the best possible audio resolution and the most features. At this point, avoid audio cards that limit resolution to 16 bits at 44.1 kHz, in favor of cards that allow for at least resolutions up to 24 bits at 96 kHz—24/192 is even better. Productions in the immediate future will demand these specifications.

Digital audio cards and interfaces have taken on a different character in recent years. The original audio cards inserted into the internal computer slots were relatively slow and offered very few features.

Current high-powered audio interfaces still typically connect via an internal PCI or other high-speed expansion bus. Sometimes the card contains the processing power with the audio inputs and outputs located on the card itself. More frequently, the card acts as the link to a hardware processor, which is typically a rack-mounted device that contains impressive processing power to augment the computer system.

Modern interfaces are often connected to the central computer via FireWire. These interfaces have brought vast increases in simplicity and flexibility. They don't require additional internal cards to access the data bus, so they are unparalleled in their simplicity and convenience. In fact some interfaces, like the Digidesign Mbox and the MOTU Traveler, are powered by the host computer. If you use a laptop and record any field or location audio, this is an absolute bonus. These devices are small, lightweight, and they sound good. The only downside of these bus-powered devices is that they often provide fewer audio channels than other types and they add a drain on your laptop computer battery, but the advantages they offer are amazing.

Tactile Control Surfaces for Digital Workstations

If you have everything happening on your computer and you're frustrated by constantly reaching for the mouse and clicking on small pictures of knobs and faders, check out the newest tactile controllers on the block. For not too much cash, you can work on a manual control surface that feels like a mixer but accesses the full power of the digital and MIDI domain. It brings the comfort of an analog mixer into the bliss of digital flexibility.

Be sure the control surface manufacturer offers expansion options. If you like having eight channels of faders, buttons, and knobs, you might really like having 16, 32, or more.

Combining MIDI and Live Recording

With the development of digital recording software that also sequences MIDI data, home recording has changed radically. I'm really a drummer who has played a lot of guitar and bass, so I've been forced to grow in my keyboard skills to even sequence the most basic synth and piano parts. In the years since MIDI software became available, I've sequenced the piano and rhythm tracks for several albums and other commercial projects. I've been able to get by, but once I was given the tools to record my guitar parts right along with the sequenced tracks, life changed for me. Plus, I could lay down vocals, percussion, and anything else I wanted. It was like a musical revival all over again. Even though I had the tools to sync my multitrack to my computer, the control and flexibility offered by the complete digital/MIDI software was amazing.

Music is changing all the time. The exciting thing about the phenomenal growth of technology is the creative freedom it provides. Most musicians feel more relaxed and emotionally free when they're at home than when they're in the studio performing under the pressure of the record light, the producer, or the clock.

Sometimes the realization of the hourly rate stifles the creative flow. Only the most seasoned studio musicians come alive in the studio environment—and then somebody else is probably paying for the time anyway. The creative environment in the home studio should release and increase the depth of modern music. We all benefit.

Depending on the musical style, it's common to record real guitar, grand piano, vocals, and solo instruments over a basic MIDI sequence that includes drums, percussion, bass, and synths. Sometimes, simply adding a sax or guitar solo over a well-produced sequence brings new life to the whole project. With the ease of integration between MIDI and digital recording, we hear any combination of recording processes all the time. In this era, we can pick and choose the techniques and instruments that work best for the music, easily combining them all at home. We might be limited by access to proficient musicians to play the parts we need, but the recording tools aren't the problem anymore.

mLAN

mLAN stands for *music local area network*. Developed by Yamaha, it is a FireWire-based open protocol designed specifically as a newer and much more powerful substitute for standard MIDI protocol. It provides for high-speed transmission and control of multiple audio channels, effects parameters, and MIDI data, as well as very powerful interconnectivity between all mLAN devices on the network.

Essentially, this protocol makes all of your mLAN equipment operate together like one unit. All connections, whether audio, effects, transport, or routing, are made through FireWire—no additional cables are required. Digital mixers, combined through mLAN, share channels and processing. Keyboards have access to external effects devices, and audio channels have access to keyboard effects. This is really a rather powerful protocol.

All devices connect simultaneously via a single ASIO or CoreAudio driver, as if the entire setup was a single device. The MIDI and audio signal flow may be routed freely, and data can be stored without reconfiguring cable connections. All connections occur through the FireWire cables. A computer is not needed for any interconnectivity of mLAN devices—it is merely an optional hub capable of adding more power to the network.

Yamaha designed mLAN as a non-proprietary open protocol, so virtually any manufacturer can easily access and incorporate it into their devices. In addition, it employs and extends the popular IEEE 1394 FireWire protocol—one of the favored and powerful new-generation data communication standards. Yamaha has made it easy for manufacturers to jump into the mLAN alliance. Although many manufacturers have been reluctant to switch from standard MIDI to the newer mLAN protocol, it's inevitable that network communications and device interactivity must grow with technological and artistic needs.

MIDI Production Techniques

This chapter gives instructions, suggestions, and insight regarding MIDI sequencing. Equipment is not the main problem most inexperienced recordists face. Modern gear is typically capable of very sophisticated production. Knowing how to optimize the use of modern equipment to create wonderfully inspired music is the key to musical success and gratification. The information I offer here is from my experience with music and equipment. Across the board, I've seen these techniques and tricks make a difference in both sound quality and emotional power of the recording projects with which I've been involved.

Constructing MIDI Drum Parts

One of the first things I learned about commercial music was that a band is only as good as its drummer. The same concept holds true in the MIDI sequencing world. A sequence is only as good as its drum and percussion tracks. If you build a sequence on a foundation made of loose clay, you're in a heap of trouble. If you construct a foundation that's solid granite, finely sculpted, and shaped to support the framework in all the right places, you have a chance at greatness.

I'll usually find the stylistically appropriate feel for the song, develop a reference groove, and then, after the arrangement comes together, I refine the drum part so it fits with the bass and the other ingredients. Everything needs to work together to create a musical representation that's precise, exciting, and full of emotion.

The Groove

Once you decide on the perfect rhythmic feel for your music, you've begun to build the road to satisfaction. However, one of the biggest problems for many recordists new to sequencing is the drum track. If you don't have a clue what the drums typically do in the style of music you like to create, you need to do your homework. Most musical styles use a few characteristic drum grooves over and over with some variations for fills and rhythm section interaction. Listen to Audio Example 8-1. Notice the difference in the feel of each drum groove. In most cases, it's obvious even to the untrained ear which stylistic family each groove belongs to.

Audio Example 8-1

Several Drum Grooves

Music never has been—and never will be—a stagnant means of expression. Even in music that stays within stylistic borders, there's constant change. Sometimes the change comes in the form of a wild, new, exciting twist that is fresh and alive to all who experience it. Sometimes it comes as a fresh look at a previously used approach. It's up to each of us to jump completely into the music we love, staying in it for the long haul. Even as our likes and dislikes change over the years, there's always a chance that what is out of style will come back into style and that we'll become the experts on the latest rage.

There's nothing like an authentic groove, and there's nothing quite as bad as a poor imitation—a groove wannabe. Figure out what it takes to get the perfect groove together for your music. Maybe that means you should avoid sequencing and you really should hire a skilled professional to provide the rock-solid foundation your music deserves.

During a serious recording effort, a lot of energy is spent finding the right feel. Listen to several different styles of music and describe how they make you feel. Some will probably make you feel on edge, some will make you feel relaxed, some might create a feeling of agitation or irritation, some might make you happy, and some might make you sad. Go down the list of emotions and states of mind—you'll probably be able to find music to evoke each one. Your mission here is to find some techniques that will help provide the appropriate foundation for the emotion inspired by the music you're recording.

The groove is the feel of a musical performance. It consists of such considerations as beat placement, accent placement, accent emphasis, note lengths, chord lengths, rhythmic interactions, emotional passion, and instrumentation.

Groove Quantize

Quantization isn't always a sterile technique reserved for techno-mania. When properly applied, it helps solidify the framework of the music. Through tasteful applications of quantize strength and sensitivity and through careful beat placement, sequenced drum and percussion parts can be very supportive and downright exciting.

Groove quantize is one feature of modern sequencers that is particularly useful in developing and consistently recreating specific musical feels. This type of quantizing lets you determine the specifications of the quantize grid. If you want beats two and four to push slightly ahead of the beat, you simply access the master grid, setting those beats to whatever position works. In addition, groove quantize includes a customized accent scheme; if you want to accent all the offbeats, simply set the accents in the groove grid. This way any time a track is quantized, even by 100 percent, the beats line up with the customized grid position and accent scheme. Listen to Audio Examples 8-2 through 8-5 for examples that illustrate the difference a groove makes.

Audio Example 8-2
100-Percent Quantize

Audio Example 8-3
Groove Quantize 1

Audio Example 8-4
Groove Quantize 2

Audio Example 8-5
Groove Quantize 3

Drum Set Patterns

If you've been avoiding creating your own drum patterns because you haven't quite been able to understand drum parts, now is the time to take the step toward rhythmic freedom. The essentials of drum patterns are simple; the complexities of drum virtuosity are astonishing! Commercial music styles are based on simple drum patterns—patterns and concepts that can be understood and felt by the masses. You don't need to be a virtuoso to understand and create drum patterns that work, and work well.

Most commercial drum patterns are in common time (four beats per measure), and the vast majority include a snare drum on beats two and four. The kick drum might play on beats one and three, on all four beats, or often on any combination of eighth or sixteenth notes. What the kick drum does largely depends on the bass guitar part. The two instruments must work together to form a solid foundation. The right hand typically provides the background unit for the groove—either straight eighth notes, sixteenth notes, or quarter notes. The left foot usually plays on beats two and four, along with the snare. Listen to

Common Drum Patterns

Most commercial drum patterns are in common time (four beats per measure) and, for the large majority, include a snare drum on beats two and four. The kick drum might play on beats one and three, on all four beats, or often on any combination of eighth or sixteenth notes. What the kick drum does is largely dependent on the bass guitar part. Often, the kick drum and bass guitar rhythms are identical.

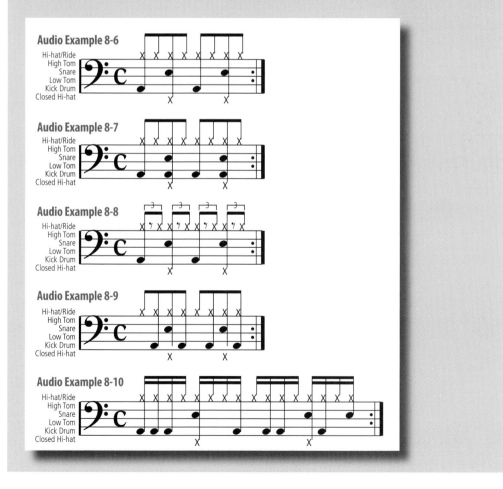

Audio Examples 8-6 through 8-10 to hear examples of different drum patterns.

Audio Example 8-6

Kick on 1 and 3 Groove

Audio Example 8-7

Kick on All Four Beats

Audio Example 8-8

Kick on 1 and 3 (Swing)

Audio Example 8-9

Kick on All Off Beats

Audio Example 8-10

Kick on Various Sixteenth Notes

The previous patterns don't represent all styles by any means, but they offer the basis for much of what happens in most mainstream commercial styles. In country music and some rock styles, these patterns could cover the essence of 95 percent of the drum parts on a given album. As the musical style becomes more rhythmically complex and aggressive, the drum patterns likewise become more rhythmically complex and aggressive.

Listen to Audio Examples 8-11 through 8-15. Notice how the drum patterns relate to the previous set. You might feel they're more interesting, or you might think they're kind of busy and confusing—personal taste and musical preference dictate the opinion. Style and emotional requirements indicate their musical relevance.

Audio Example 8-11

Drum Example 1

More Complex Drum Patterns

Notice how these drum patterns relate to the previous set. You might feel they're more interesting or you might think they're kind of busy and confusing—it all depends on your personal taste and musical preference. Style and emotional requirements indicate their musical relevance.

Typically, the more complex the drum pattern, the more important it is that the entire rhythm section plays with great precision. Sloppy performances of complex rhythms usually results in groove pandemonium.

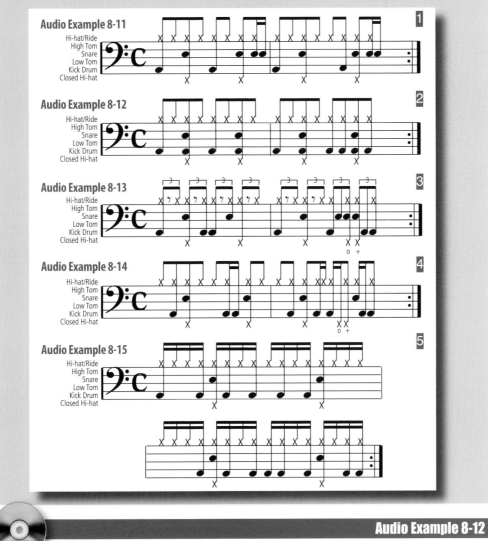

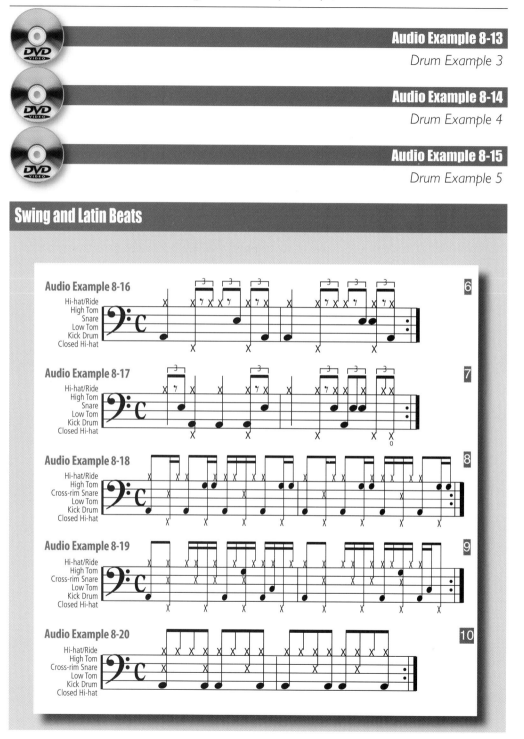

Audio Example 8-13

Drum Example 3

Audio Example 8-14

Drum Example 4

Audio Example 8-15

Drum Example 5

Swing and Latin Beats

Audio Example 8-16

Audio Example 8-17

Audio Example 8-18

Audio Example 8-19

Audio Example 8-20

A pattern that's more complex is by no means better or worse than a pattern that's simple. Young drummers are always trying to play the most complicated stuff. More seasoned drummers have learned that drums are all about maintaining a rock-solid foundation; therefore, an experienced player usually selects a fairly simple and clean pattern to support the musical vision. A great drummer has the depth and technique to maintain an undeniable groove, even through musically tasteful and well-placed fills and embellishments.

Swing and Latin patterns are typically more complex, although most grooves maintain a pulse that revolves around a common time kick, snare, kick, snare pattern. Audio Examples 8-16 through 8-20 illustrate the relationship of the more complicated patterns to the more basic patterns.

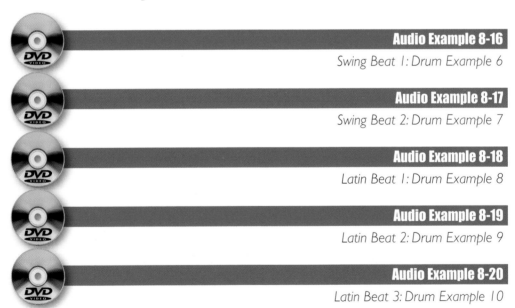

Audio Example 8-16

Swing Beat 1: Drum Example 6

Audio Example 8-17

Swing Beat 2: Drum Example 7

Audio Example 8-18

Latin Beat 1: Drum Example 8

Audio Example 8-19

Latin Beat 2: Drum Example 9

Audio Example 8-20

Latin Beat 3: Drum Example 10

Practice creating the drum patterns in the previous Audio Examples, and then take them to the next level. Change the kick and snare drum a little, and vary the right-hand pattern. Or, try something a little different.

Always think creatively. These example drum patterns should provide a basis for confidence and experimentation.

Accents

Drum parts are often full of dynamic changes and great passionate outbursts. Don't overlook the power of dynamics and rhythmic accents in your drum creations. It's typically the accents that really define the emotional impact of music. With drum sequences, you can either play the accents in when you originally program the parts, or you can simply turn an instrument up in volume for a period of time. Experiment with placement of accents within your drum grooves.

Listen to Audio Examples 8-21 through 8-23. Notice that even though each example contains the identical rhythm, the feels are markedly different.

Audio Example 8-21

Accents 1

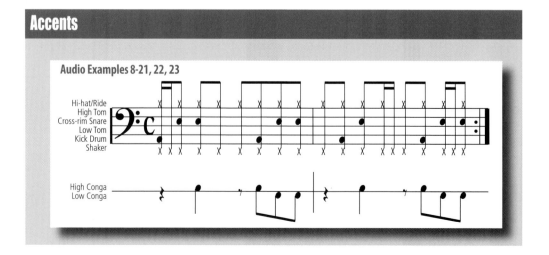

Audio Example 8-22

Accents 2

Audio Example 8-23

Accents 3

Fills

Listen to some of your favorite music in the style you're recording to experience the appropriate types of drum fills. Analyze the fills; try to duplicate the rhythmic feel of each. Drum fills typically include toms but often include snare or even kick drums. The king of tom fills is simply four sixteenth notes on each of four toms, for a total of four beats (a full measure), ending in a crash (listen to Audio Example 8-24). Young drummers feel like they've arrived when they get the roll around the toms down.

Audio Example 8-24

The King of Tom Fills

Unfortunately, a simple sixteenth-note pattern around the toms usually sounds rigid and mundane in a sequencer. It's possible to creatively add accents to a measure of sixteenth notes to spice things up, but it never sounds as cool sequenced as it does when a real drummer plays it on real drums. Part of the problem with sampled drum sounds resides in the consistent attack sound. A real drum played with

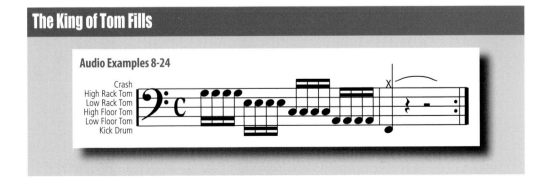

The King of Tom Fills

Audio Examples 8-24

Crash
High Rack Tom
Low Rack Tom
High Floor Tom
Low Floor Tom
Kick Drum

drumsticks varies greatly from attack to attack because of the variations in speed, attack area, and other human inconsistencies. Some software manufacturers allow for variable samples depending on attack velocity and other assignable random considerations. An option like this really adds an authentic edge to drum sequences.

In most cases, it's best to keep fills as simple as possible. A simple "da dum dum crash" might be the perfect drum fill, whereas a "buddley buddley buddley boom wackiticky brrrrrrrr snap" will probably get in the way and sound silly. With the ability to record fills at a slow tempo—to be played back at a fast tempo—it's easy to get carried away and create a drum fill that could never be performed by a live drummer. A drum fill should always support the flow from one musical section to the next. Flashy fills for the sake of flash alone have no place in good music. However, flashy fills that build and support the emotional feel of the song are awesome. An unrealistic fill combined with a constant attack makes for distraction, rather than emotion-filled support.

Drum fills are typically placed at the end of a musical section, leading into the next section. However, they don't need to lead into each section. Sometimes the drums serve the music better by simply playing through a section change with no fill. Other times, a simple crash at the beginning of a section is all that's needed. Taste and discipline should guide your decisions about fills. It's always better to understate fills than it is to stick in too many.

Listen to Audio Examples 8-25 through 8-28 for simple fills that work well in the context of sequencing.

Fills

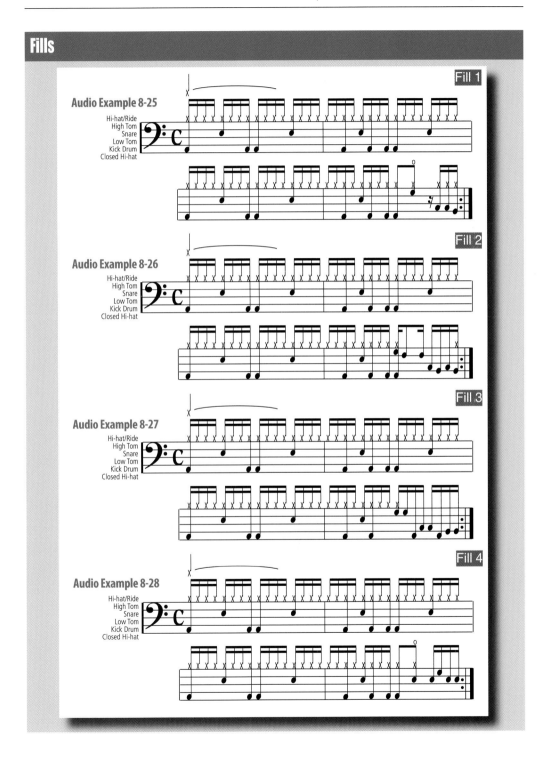

Audio Example 8-25
Groove into Fill 1

Audio Example 8-26
Groove into Fill 2

Audio Example 8-27
Groove into Fill 3

Audio Example 8-28
Groove into Fill 4

Believability

If you'd really like to create drum patterns that sound like a real drummer played them—and those are the best kind—keep in mind that drummers are people, too. They usually don't have more than two arms and two legs. Therefore, they can't play the cymbals while they rip off a huge tom fill; they can't usually play fast sixteenths on the ride cymbal and hi-hat while performing an intricately syncopated snare-kick combination with tom fills included. Envision a drummer playing the drum parts you devise. If you can visualize a drummer playing the part, your patterns will probably sound authentic.

If you have an excellent sense of time or if you're a fine drummer, try inputting the drums in real time. Avoid quantizing just to see how the patterns feel. Sometimes this approach works well, but you really must be able to play the parts right in the pocket, and that's not always easy to do. I've had some success at real-time drum programming, especially after the rest of the ingredients have been entered and finalized, but I usually find that even a slight degree of quantizing cleans up everything very well.

Construction

Construction and performance of a drum part are much more natural—the beats flow in a much more musical way—when the rest of the arrangement has been put together. I typically use a reference groove (a one- or two-bar pattern that indicates the correct feel) to build the sequence around. Then, once everything is in place, I'll go back through the entire song, playing the kick and snare together first; I find these two ingredients fundamental in the way they interact with the rest of the arrangement. Once I'm satisfied with the kick-snare combination, I add the hi-hat, ride cymbal, and crash cymbal parts—in one pass if possible. I like to add the tom fills last so I can tell where they're really needed.

Percussion Patterns

Percussion instruments really add the frosting to the groove cake. A simple shaker can propel a drum pattern. The constant action of an eighth- or sixteenth-note shaker part provides momentum that might not otherwise exist. Experiment with shifting percussion parts forward and back in time relation to the rest of the pattern—use the smallest increment available. Notice the changes in the feel of the following patterns as I move the shaker ahead of and behind the rest of the groove.

Audio Example 8-29
Groove and Shaker

Audio Example 8-30
Shaker ahead of the Groove

Audio Example 8-31
Shaker behind the Groove

Try the same techniques on tambourines, clavés, cowbells, hand claps, triangles, or any other percussion instrument.

Audio Examples 8-32 through 8-34 demonstrate some popular uses for common percussion instruments. Listen to several recordings that include percussion; see whether you hear any of these parts.

Audio Example 8-32
Tambourine

Audio Example 8-33
Cowbell

Audio Example 8-34
Conga

Many Percussion Instruments

There are many percussion instruments; there are hundreds of commercially manufactured percussion instruments readily available. Any number of multiculturally inspired drums can be found, along with all sorts of metal clanging, thunking, popping, boinging, tinkling, and crashing instruments. Any instrument that is struck is a percussion instrument, including instruments in the piano family because the hammers strike the strings. If you ever hire a professional percussionist for a session, you'll soon find the studio littered with stuff.

Percussionists are notorious for turning everything into a musical instrument. Keys, beads, pop cans, coffee cups, automobile brake drums, circular saw blades, and chunks of metal and wood are all common percussion instruments. It's incredible how a tasteful percussionist can add unique character that's full of life to a recording.

Simple Parts That Work Together

Be sure to keep percussion parts simple. It's best to create a couple very simple percussion parts that work together well. Throughout your drum set and percussion programming adventure, you'll find the greatest success in creating simple musical parts that support the flow and emotion of the music. Experiment with the points I've highlighted in this chapter.

The art of drum programming demands practice, as well as a thorough understanding of style, musical taste, and creativity. When those ingredients are combined in proper proportion, your music has the chance it deserves to be heard.

Forming the Bass Line

The bass and drum parts should work together so tightly that they could almost be considered one part. The bass guitar and kick drum often play the identical rhythm; if they don't, they must at least complement one another. Listen to Audio Examples 8-35 through 8-38. Pay particular attention to the way the bass guitar and kick drum support each other.

Audio Example 8-35

Kick and Bass 1

Audio Example 8-36

Kick and Bass 2

Audio Example 8-37

Kick and Bass 3

Audio Example 8-38

Kick and Bass 4

Patterns

The most common chord tones used in bass line construction are the root and fifth of the associated scale. When a bass guitar line flows through passing tones, it's important to use the proper scales. Because this part is so foundational to a song, it almost always sounds best to keep the bass line simple, rhythmically and melodically. To add flow to a bass line, especially leading into a phrase, it's pretty common to go through the sixth and seventh notes of the scale. It's also common to walk up the scale to the next chord.

These techniques are common to most styles; what changes most is the bass sound. The playing approach is so different from style to style that the resulting sound, feel, and emotion vary dramatically. When you are sequencing a bass part, always take into consideration the playing techniques used by most bass players active in the particular musical style.

The Groove

As with drums and percussion, the bass needs to lock into the stylistically correct groove. If you have quantized the drums to a customized groove, it's important that the bass be quantized to the same groove. Audio Example 8-39 demonstrates the bass and drums in and out of the same groove.

Audio Example 8-39

In and Out of the Groove

Reality/Believability

As soon as synthesized bass lines became a usable option, music programmers started to push the bass range envelope. A standard four-string bass guitar has a finite range—from E1 (41.2 Hz) to about D4 (293.66 Hz). A synthesizer is not bound by those limitations, so especially in the low end, bass notes started to edge their way to the basement. Low D, C, and even B soon worked their way into contemporary sound.

When synth bass first came into being, we were still bound by the limitation of vinyl records and an evolving cassette technology, so it was held that recordings were more universally acceptable if the bass parts stayed within the bounds of the standard four-string. As CDs and other digital formats became the standard, and with the advent of much-improved consumer audio, those low notes became more and more fun to listen to, so they became more and more common. Life for the bass player was about to change. Most active bassists now carry a five-string bass with a string added to the low end, extending the range down to low B0 (30.87 Hz).

Feel

Depending on the musical style, it might be appropriate to shift the bass guitar forward or back in time, relative to the drums. In certain jazz applications, the bass is right on the front edge of the beat, helping drive the momentum. Other styles require the bass to land precisely on the beat with the drums, or even behind the beat for a more laid back feel. Different personality characteristics absolutely transfer to musical interpretation and feel. A hyper person tends to play ahead of the beat and creates a unique tension in the music. A laid back personality relaxes a groove. The highly skilled and experienced professional can adjust the temperament of a performance to fit the desired effect for the musical application. Because you have the sequencer at your disposal, you only need the knowledge of the effect created by variance in performance and feel. You can direct the computer to adjust the placement of each beat for the perfect blend of aggressive and passive emotion. Cool, huh?

Guitar Parts

It's sometimes difficult for pianists to create an authentic-sounding guitar part. The guitar has certain pitch and voicing limitations dictated by the physical design of the instrument. The range of the guitar is from E2 (82.41 Hz) to as high as E6 (1318.51 Hz). The strings stack up from the lowest E (the sixth string) in fourths, except for a major third interval between the second and third strings.

Believability

Part of the guitar sound comes from the characteristic voicings, which are comfortably played on the guitar, although they might be difficult to play on a keyboard. To create authentic-sounding guitar parts, you must use authentic chord voicings. The other idiomatic trait that makes the guitar unique is the strum. Chords are not played all at once; they're either strummed up or down. Good players adjust their pick speed to create differing comp feels, but even at the fastest pick speed chords are slightly arpeggiated. Some software packages include an option to simulate the guitarist's strum, but the same feel can be accomplished through a stylistically correct keyboard performance.

The Groove

Guitar relates to the groove completely on a stylistic basis. Imagine the personality of the music, and you'll find the guitar groove. Funky guitar comps are often right on top of the beat; they lock tightly in with the drums and bass, almost becoming a part of the percussion section. A lot of fast country music is driven by the guitarist's aggressive and flamboyant energy. Picture a grunge rock group—although the music is almost always guitar-driven, the guitar parts are often rhythmically laid back. There are exceptions to all these points, but the key issue is that styles differ in their rhythmic emphasis.

Patterns

There are countless guitar strum patterns, but if you're really trying to create authentic-sounding guitar parts, always keep in mind that the guitarist strums up and down for fast notes. Often the downbeats are all down strokes and the upbeats are all up strokes. Even if a measure contains all upbeats, the guitarist would probably play all up strokes simply to stay in the flow of the groove.

Guitarists also use slides, bends, and grace notes in a completely different way than a keyboard. A synth pitch bend is not the same as a guitar note bend or slide. Whereas a keyboardist bends the entire keyboard through a continuously variable pitch range, a guitarist often bends one note while holding another steady. A guitarist's grace notes and hammer-ons typically contain discrete steps through a chromatic or diatonic tone set—especially when played within a chord comp. Therefore, to accurately reproduce a fingered slide, the keyboardist must adjust the synth pitch bend to chromatically notch through a pitch range. In addition, many of the chord comps need to lead in with a grace note or a set of grace notes that could actually be played by a guitarist.

Grand and Electric Piano Parts

The Groove

Piano adds a distinct fullness to an arrangement. Sometimes the piano adds such a fullness that it distracts from the rest of the arrangement. In a commercial style, it's rare to hear the piano just going for it. The piano parts are typically finely crafted to lend support at the right times and to release space and openness when it's needed for the other instruments. Like the guitar, piano is style-driven. Given an old time rock 'n' roll song, the piano is probably off and running, leading the whole band. Given a contemporary pop ballad, the piano might be laid back beyond belief. Most of the time, an up-tempo piano comp blends in with the percussion and bass guitar to form solid rhythmic and harmonic support for the rest of the instruments.

Patterns

Most singer/songwriters who play and write on the piano fill out the sound so much on the piano that there's no room for any other instruments in the orchestration. They get used to playing constant eighth- or sixteenth-note patterns and arpeggios. These kinds of parts usually need to be set aside to make room for the rest of the instrumentation. Sometimes in a pop commercial ballad, the piano is the primary source of rhythm and harmony, but in the regular world of popular styles, piano parts are very simple and supportive until the perfect musical moment, and then they add sparkle in a way that no other instrument really can.

Listen to the following Audio Examples. Notice how the piano gets in the way in Audio Example 8-40 and how it supports the emotion in Audio Example 8-41.

Audio Example 8-40
Piano in the Way

Audio Example 8-41
Piano Supporting the Song

Grand Pianos versus Rhodes Pianos

The choice between grand pianos and Rhodes sounds is subject to application and taste. Typically, grand pianos are used on aggressive rock or country songs and on big pop ballads. Rhodes piano sounds are more commonly used as a mellow support on mid-tempo middle-of-the-road songs and on mellow ballads. Their sound qualities support these applications, but they both add their own unique personality to whatever music they're included in. Experiment. The choice is yours, and it will be the right choice if it's based on emotion and passion for your song.

Some pieces of music don't call for piano at all. The more experienced you become at producing, orchestrating, and arranging, the more selective you'll become in your orchestration choices.

Believability

The sequencer provides the opportunity to build piano parts that could only be performed by a 15- or 20-fingered pianist. Across the board in any instrumental part you sequence, it's best to keep the ingredients simple and potentially playable in a live setting. Building parts that are too complicated to play quickly distracts far more than it supports.

Piano requires great care in quantizing. Because pianists tend to roll chords—instead of just pounding the notes all at once—and because the melodic support is typically very expressive, quantizing in any degree has the potential to destroy the performance. If the piano performance comes from an accomplished pianist, try to avoid quantizing. Quantize only to solidify the musical groove, and only quantize in the measures that really need it. Always copy the MIDI piano part to another track before you start to quantize; leave the original untouched. If you keep the original performance intact, you can always go back to it later if you realize the track had more life before you started to fix it.

Feel

Especially when the piano is the main instrument, its feel is amazingly crucial to a song's development and stylistic impact. Shifting the piano in time makes a huge difference in the feel of the song. The touch of the performer and the use of accents, phrasing, and nuance comprise the piano's powerful musical influence. Piano is one of the easiest instruments to ruin through the sequencing process. A simple, emotion-filled performance usually serves the musical needs of a song best.

The Frosting

Once the basic rhythm-section tracks are together and working for the needs of the song, it's time to consider ways to increase the impact through effective orchestrating and arranging. If the rhythm section parts have all been crafted to work together in a musically supportive way, the need for additional parts, such as strings, brass, and sound effects, might be minimal. Young musicians tend to keep adding ingredients, hoping that more sounds will add up to a cooler sound. In truth, the opposite usually occurs. The more you add, the less important and the more hidden everything is. It's very possible to fill a song up with sound, and then realize that nothing sounds close, important, or intimate.

Listen to your rhythm tracks and vocals. Set up a good punchy mix, and then look for spots that seem empty or lack emotion. Take notes on exactly where you feel the music is texturally needy. Then, before you start adding parts, tinker with the mix at those spots; see whether there's already a musical ingredient that would fill each spot wonderfully if it were simply turned up for a few beats or measures. Try to fill in the song with what you have first. If you need to add some fills, pads, or effects, do so with authority and resolve, but be certain each part is necessary.

Audio Example 8-42

Three Mixes: Bare Bones, Some Stuff, Lots of Stuff

Strings and Pads

String sections and synth pads are commonly used in most styles. We've already covered layering and combining sound modules in this book, so I'll assume you can find the perfect sound for your song. Once you have the sound ready to go—the sound that brings out the best in your music—finding the perfect place to use it is the key. The problem with most synth pads is that they sound so huge and massively warm and inviting that once you start playing them, it's hard to stop.

In most cases, the musical flow is better supported if the pad comes in at key points and then disappears until it's really needed again. When a huge pad sound stops, the space needs to be filled by something else. The ingredient is usually already in the mix; it simply needs to be turned up.

Listen to Audio Example 8-43. Notice how empty the orchestration is when the pad goes away. Then listen to Audio Example 8-44. Notice how the acoustic guitar comes up to fill the hole left by the pad.

Audio Example 8-43

Empty When Pad Leaves

Audio Example 8-44

Acoustic Guitar Comes in to Fill Hole

Pad sounds don't always need to be played as chords. Some of the most effective string and pad lines begin as single notes, building to more notes as the arrangement grows. Try waiting until the middle of the second verse or so; then, bring the pad in on a single note line that starts in the lower (cello) register, moving up and controlling the flow into the second chorus. In the chorus, break into a multi-note pad. You might find this technique really highlights and builds the song. Or it might not work at all—that's the beauty of music.

Audio Example 8-45

Single Line Pad

Brass

Used in just the right way, brass sounds add sparkle and life to the right musical style. If you'd like to sequence brass parts so they sound like a brass section, you must research arranging techniques. A brass section that sounds great live is always performing excellent arrangements, using powerful and characteristically appropriate voicings. The players are probably very talented, and they are able to lock into the groove in a way that propels the music to a new level. Excellent brass parts are dependent upon inspired articulation, dynamics, phrasing, and emotion. If you're unfamiliar with these stylistic ingredients, it will be difficult for you to create brass parts that work well.

Listen to some hit songs in the style you're recording. Analyze the brass parts for their melodic, rhythmic, and dynamic content. Try to play the brass parts from several well-produced songs. This will give you some insight into what good brass parts are.

Be sure that once you begin constructing brass parts, you avoid laying the brass over the vocals. It's usually okay to let the brass play some short punches during the verse or chorus because these kinds of parts become very percussive and can support the feel. Longer, more melodic brass parts that include the entire section should be used carefully to avoid conflicting with the melodic vocals. Lower trombone and French horn lines—especially unison lines—don't conflict when they're written in a way that supports the melodic flow. When arranged correctly, they act more as string or pad supports than they do as brass highlights.

Sound Effects

With the onset of samplers and other digital manipulation tools, almost any sound can show up as a musical ingredient. Sounds are amazing in their diversity and flexibility. The tasteful use of sound effects and unique samples can bring new life and momentum to a musical work, but it can also distract from the purpose of the music. Some producers like to put a different sound in each musical hole or break. This was really popular in the '80s and early '90s. Although this technique can continue to give the listener something to draw him or her back to the tune, music that offers an excellent performance and enticing lyrics can have longevity and a greater impact with which to draw in the listener.

Combining MIDI and Live Recording

With the development of digital recording software that also sequences MIDI data, home recording has changed radically. I'm really a drummer who has played a lot of guitar and bass, so I've been forced to grow in my keyboard skills to even sequence the most basic synth and piano parts. In the years since MIDI software became available, I've sequenced the piano and rhythm tracks for several albums and other commercial projects. I've been able to get by, but once I was given the tools to record my guitar parts right along with the sequenced tracks, life changed for me. Plus, I could lay down vocals, percussion, and anything else I wanted. It was like a musical revival all over again. Even though I had the tools to sync my multitrack to my computer, the control and flexibility offered by the complete digital/MIDI software was amazing.

Music is changing all the time. The exciting thing about the phenomenal growth of technology is the creative freedom it provides. Most musicians feel more relaxed and emotionally free when they're at home than when they're in the studio performing under the pressure of the record light, the producer, or the clock. Sometimes the realization of the hourly rate stifles the creative flow. Only the most seasoned studio musicians come alive in the studio environment—and then somebody else is probably paying for the time anyway. The creative environment in the home studio should release and increase the depth of modern music. We all benefit.

Depending on the musical style, it's common to record real guitar, grand piano, vocals, and solo instruments over a basic MIDI sequence that includes drums, percussion, bass, and synths. Sometimes simply adding a sax or guitar solo over a well-produced sequence brings new life to the whole project. With the ease of integration between MIDI and digital recording, you hear any combination of recording processes all the time. In this era, you can pick and choose the techniques and instruments that work best for the music, easily combining them all at home. You might be limited by access to proficient musicians to play the parts you need, but the recording tools aren't the problem anymore.

Drum Loops

Samplers and digital recording have opened a new world for drum tracks. Sequenced drum tracks are difficult to construct in a way that has life, emotion, and groove; therefore, it soon became popular to sample a measure or two of an excellent live or previously sequenced drum pattern, looping it for the duration of the song. This technique provides a solid, almost mechanized foundation, but the song benefits from an inspired drum groove.

The problem with drum loops is not musical, it's legal. Digital technology provides you with such clean recordings of your favorite music that when you hear a great drum groove that's all by itself for a while, the temptation to sample it and then use it in your own songs is strong. The legal and moral implications of this technique are suspect. Copyright laws and the principles of right and wrong are often overlooked in the excitement of the moment. There are many commercially prerecorded drum loops available. CDs are available that are produced solely with drum grooves created for sampling purposes. Most sampling manufacturers have many presampled and prelooped drum tracks available for use with their products. The grooves are available without infringing on anyone's rights of ownership and hard work.

No formula works every time. Anything you hear regarding the development of your music should be taken as a suggestion. Music is such a personal and creative art form that, thankfully, there are no absolutes. Always strive to stretch the boundaries of musical styles and conformities. Use assumed truths about music to help build music that has integrity. Much of what you'll hear about musical considerations comes from years of experimentation by musicians—players as passionate as anyone about creativity and individuality. Take advantage of their experience, and then take it a little further.

Index